Women Empowerment

Giving the Power Back to the Women of Today

(A Short Insight to the History of Women in the Society)

Joanna Tracy

Published By **Chris David**

Joanna Tracy

All Rights Reserved

Women Empowerment: Giving the Power Back to the Women of Today (A Short Insight to the History of Women in the Society)

ISBN   978-1-77485-616-1

Legal & Disclaimer

The information contained in this ebook is not designed to replace or take the place of any form of medicine or professional medical advice. The information in this ebook has been provided for educational & entertainment purposes only.

The information contained in this book has been compiled from sources deemed reliable, and it is accurate to the best of the Author's knowledge; however, the Author cannot guarantee its accuracy and validity and cannot be held liable for any errors or omissions. Changes are periodically made to this book. You must consult your doctor or get professional medical advice before using any of the suggested remedies, techniques, or information in this book.

Upon using the information contained in this book, you agree to hold harmless the Author from and against any damages, costs, and expenses, including any legal fees potentially resulting from the application of any of the information provided by this guide. This disclaimer applies to any damages or injury caused by the use and application, whether directly or indirectly, of any advice or information presented, whether for breach of contract, tort, negligence, personal injury, criminal intent, or under any other cause of action.

You agree to accept all risks of using the information presented inside this book. You need to consult a professional medical practitioner in order to ensure you are both able and healthy enough to participate in this program.

Table of Contents

Introduction

What is the reason it's not acceptable to wear a skirt in your community? Why is it dangerous to go at a bar? What is the reason you don't get the same wages like the guys do? What's wrong with you to weigh a lot? or go out with no bra? What makes you think it's a flaw in your?

Women from all over the globe have been for a long time demanding equality, equal pay, equal treatment.

All women across the globe need to be acknowledged for our amazing and diverse abilities. In the words of Diane Marie child defined us, "a woman is the complete circle. In her is the capacity to invent, nurture and change."

I would like to inform that, as women, we have been blessed with internal strength, passion strength, generosity and love in order to enjoy our life fully and contribute to the world more beautiful. But if we choose only focusing on these inherent gifts however, we might not be able transmit our values to the world or just be ignored.

Why should women be afraid to bow in front of the males since it is us who make them come alive! You should agree with me that we should empower women so that they can also stand where men are, and that they can speak at the same time and in the same place that men speak, and are able to voice their opinions whenever they want to and when men do similar things and not remain there, but also take action to make choices that can create a world that is more livable and more peaceful.

It is essential to put our women on an accessible and powerful platform which will allow women to be heard, be respected, and to participate in the conditions they live in , as well as beyond the boundaries of.

Fortunately, we are moving away from the primitive belief that women shouldn't be granted key roles within their communities; are not able to speak up for themselves or be the person we want to be or do what we like or do roles that are appealing to us regardless of what the world tells us that we should not. It is time to join hands and form a sisterhood which will allow our voices to be heard further.

There are many ways to build that impressive platform for us. We are educated and we can make crafty skills and we're in love for ourselves, and we have confidence in the things brings to the table. I'll remind you one that we're a complete circle.

In her collection of poetry Sun and flower, Rupi Kaur says "I sit on the sacrifices made by one million women right before me and think about what I can do to increase the height of this mountain so that the women following me will be able to see further." My book represents my small contribution to that mountain. I wish that the beautiful women who follow me will be able to see further and more living a happy life and make the world a little more comfortable for all.

Chapter 1: Why There Are A Myriad Of Reasons To

If the future isn't female I'm not interested in it. We decide the future, however, often it does not go our way. I've experienced what it's like to look into your mirror, and be overweight and unimportant and ugly. I've been there. like to be locked in the bathroom and want to end the process. I understand what it's like to compare your life with others and think that they're better off or live happier lives. when you are unhappy and hate the body you see you in. I am aware of how it feels.

There are times that we are feeling lost and insecure and aren't sure who we can turn in order to feel more confident about ourselves. Certain of us are fortunate to have people like this in our lives , but many of us do not.

What do you do during those days? What can you do to redirect all your self-hate and frustration to an easier path? And most importantly how can you be loving to yourself?

There isn't an easy guideline on how to love yourself, but there are a few simple guidelines for pushing you toward this goal. The best thing we could do is to motivate you to do and help you learn how to be a better person, but only you are able to do the inner work for yourself.

Self-love can be defined as an attitude of self-love that is developed through actions that help us in our psychological, physical and spiritual growth. Self-love is having a great respect for your own wellbeing and happiness. Self-love involves taking care of your personal requirements and not devoting your wellbeing to please other people. Self-love is not accepting less than what you are entitled to.

Self-love may mean different things for every person, as there are many ways of taking care of our own self-love. Understanding what self-love should look like for you, as an individual, is essential to your mental wellbeing.

Chapter 2: Self Love Is Primarily About Speaking To And About Yourself And Your Feelings With Affection

According to the saying, if you don't feel you take care of yourself, no one will help you. When you feel you are loved this way, it is an effect on your behavior, in your life and how people view your personality. Everyone wants the high school-style pretty girl who everyone loves the feelingof, right? You're hoping to make everyone smile every time you enter the room you enter, don't you? You'd like to be loved, don't you? The first step towards that is to be a person who loves yourself.

If you are in love with yourself and you are happy, this is what happens;

Your life truly is yours. You value your opinion and thoughts, emotions and feelings over others' opinions about your life, you, and your personality.

You are aware of yourself, who you really are and what are looking for to achieve in your life. you can awaken your inner spirituality. There's no need to be in rivalries with other people, you enhance your self-development and self-worth, and work hard to show yourself to yourself only and not to anyone else. If you dress in a certain way you dress up because you like it, because you wish to feel confident with yourself. You're content and happy with your choice and do not want to challenge anyone else or to impress anyone else or make them consider you a good person.

You boost your self-worth by not accepting less, either professionally or personally. You are more willing to accept the failures you face as what they are: steps towards achieving more in your life.

When you realize the value you have in your life, you'll be able to attract peace, love and harmony and positive things to you.

How do I love myself?

I once said to a friend it's fine to be self-centered. It is important to be the first to yourself. You should do what you like and what you must do , not what is expected from other people or how they want you to behave or behave.

If you're soft-hearted it can be tempting to believe that you have to be a little more naive to please others. No! It's not your job to put the needs of others over your own.

Self-love can extend to self-care. Remember to take good care of yourself.

How can you take good care of yourself?

Exercise

Exercise is a highly advised method to keep your body and mind stress-free. It helps maintain a healthy body and a healthier mind by exercising.

Consume a balanced diet

It is better to most of the time strive to eat healthier and get rid of the junk food lifestyle, and indulge only in those cravings occasionally. Food is what you consume isn't it?

Have fun!

Relax with yourself, whether that's reading, sleeping or enjoying cooking, relaxing or even doing some meditation. Enjoy time with your buddies and go out shopping, going to clubs or embark on an adventure and travel, keep pets and so on. There are a myriad of activities you can take part in to have fun.

Set boundaries

When it comes to interaction with others, whether professional or personal you should always establish limits. It is important to let people know what you will and can't allow and what you can't and won't. This is the best way to gain self-respect.

If you establish boundaries to be clear, you'll stay clear of unnecessary drama and conflicts during family events, fun gatherings, or even at work.

Birds of a Feather gather together

The people you interact with is a method of revealing what you're about. It is important to surround yourself with women who share your values and are for your growth. Don't spend your time and energy with snakes who are willing to help you break.

Be yourself

Always be yourself. It is a fact that I cannot emphasize enough. Don't be afraid to say"no, yes I'm not interested. I'm not in the mood for that because I don't have the desire or am tired of it.

Make sure to keep your energy and attitude real. Keep your commitment to yourself, your values, your convictions and your morals.

Accept your mistakes

Tatiana has said it all "you aren't perfect, baby, since nobody's perfect however not a single one there's no one anywhere else as beautiful as you"

You're flawed! And so is the entire world as well as everyone else. However, we're all gorgeously imperfect. Your freckles are beautiful and they are beautiful, as are your moles. the birthmark you have is stunning Your amputated parts look gorgeous. Your dark complexion is celestial, and your light skin is stunning. It is important to accept the person you are you are, your character as well as your strengths and weaknesses your kindness and that tiny bad voice inside your head. You have to accept your fatness or skinniness, tiny boos or massive boobs or even in-between. Accept your curly, straight dark, brunette hairstyle, the skin and belly fat. thin thighs, thick legs.

Take a breather! Do not always criticize or judge yourself. It's okay to put in a lot of effort but fall short. If your efforts fail, gain an knowledge.

Develop your spirituality

The word "spiritual" here doesn't mean the belief in God or religion, and so on. It is the connection between you and yourself as well as others and finally, you and your surroundings.

A strong spiritual foundation will aid in developing self-growth confidence, self-worth, and self-esteem. You can awaken your spirituality by meditating and being with yourself, gaining a better understanding of your self and many other ways.

Refurbish yourself

Develop your abilities, discover new hobbies, and explore other options to discover other areas you might be skilled at.

Take time for your interests and take advantage of opportunities to increase your interest in these activities and enhance your skills and skills.

Finally, ladies, relax! Really. Get rid of those anxious and exhausting thoughts. There is more to life than the unpaid bills or deadlines at work that you have to be able to meet. Everything is in place by the passage of time. Recognize that certain events and events are out of our control.

If stressing and worry won't accomplish the task Why do you worry? Why should you be worried?

Lovely women. Hope these tips help you on your journey towards self-love and self-care. In addition, if you are doubtful of the value of your self or you are pondering the question: what is the reason I should love myself? Honey, there are many reasons to.

Conclusion

Women have to fulfill our role in the role of "women" and take action to support one another. There are many dreams and goals to make an impact in the world, but this goals are not achievable if you aren't in love with yourself or believe in your abilities. To climb a mountain, one must first begin to climb toward it.

Women have gained a lot of attention in recent years for being in positions that allow them to make decisions that people don't are able to take seriously. There is the first female vice president of America. United States, we have strong women who have made an impact on our lives, such as Opera Winfrey, Maya Angelo, Michelle Obama, and the list goes on. It's true that female presidents are also the norm in the present. Women, it's the new trend. is female!

It is not necessary to hold an official position or have authority before you are able to make an alteration. It is possible to start at the base. What can you do to achieve this? Small actions such as helping yourself and encouraging yourself, or helping and encouraging those around you.

Your friend with body insecurity issues Do not make her feel ashamed. Do your best to help her understand the truth about her being beautiful just as she is. It is important to acknowledge and celebrate our beauty and worth. However, I'll tell you to be yourself first before you convince others that you are worthy of being loved.

There are a lot of women, some of whom I've mentioned in this small book, who have come from the bottom of the barrel but are now living the most fulfilling lives today. If they're able to do it, surely you can too.

The saying goes that a woman who is successful is able to build a solid base with the stones people have put in her path. Don't be swayed by the unjustified opinions of other people, you should remain confident and remain true to your goals. We've all are all here for this. We all.

By being females and having a connection to one another that I believe is indestructible when we cement the bonds. We are capable of doing this. We are able to do it. Beautiful women, we are truly able to do it.

Chapter 3: Women Empowerment

"Women are welcome in every place in which decisions are taken. ... The rule isn't right that women are not the majority." Ruth Bader Ginsburg

Women's empowerment has been gradually gaining ground. The past of women's roles in the society is tragic. In recent years and with the advancement of technology there has been progress. But, who knows how much progress could have been achieved if inclusion of women had been initiated at the beginning.

Naturally that is the case, but bygones are bygones, and the future will be what we decide to make of it. That's why we try to educate but also take decisive steps to ensure women's empowerment in all fields, states and even at the level of the region.

There's a saying "two heads are better than one' however who's saying that the other head doesn't belong to a female? There is a world with two genders, male as well as female. To take the correct steps to please and create a safe social and environmental conditions for them , they must collaborate.

Women is a word that is plural which has a lot of power. It represents each female around the globe with a lot of potential, or simply a desire. Today, women are an untapped treasure and gold mine for all nations that are educated enough to recognize her value.

With all the greatness that is connected to the woman she is, why are we talking about women's empowerment? Empowerment is the process of empowering oneself and increasing confidence. It's about taking control of your life, and taking advantage of the rights are essential to you.

As such, women's empowerment means having access for every woman to the full spectrum of life , including education as well as justice, health career, lifestyle, and so many other things, all without prejudice. It's about giving women their rightful choices in life , and equipping them with the resources to make those decisions and confront the various social challenges of life face-to-face.

Women empowerment is about the rights of women everywhere to the full benefits accrued to her as an individual , without any discrimination or bias due to gender. It seeks to eliminate inequity, discrimination, partiality and gender-based discrimination.

As was previously stated that women are precious, it's only right to elevate their standing in the society and pay the respect they deserve. In order to ensure that they understand their importance and rights, and to ensure that they get the proper education and opportunities to understand the significance of this and make a difference in society for not only themselves, but for other people.

Which woman has the power to be empowered?

A woman who is empowered is a woman who is in her own rights, with her way of life, and in her shoes. There isn't any painting of the physical representation of what a woman empowered ought to look like or what she should be doing. The purpose of having power is to to be the person you wish to be, without discrimination. If, for instance, what you would like to be is a world-class business tycoon then you can go forward and design your own path. If all you want to accomplish is to enjoy the simplicity of life and feel at peace, then obviously, you're allowed to be that way. There is no reason to believe to the contrary.

When we speak of empowered women, the most common error and image that comes into the minds of many people is successful women. It's important to remember that the purpose of women's empowerment isn't just to pick some women to help them achieve their hopes. It's to allow every female child and every woman in the world to choose her path without discrimination, hurdles or resentment.

A young girl would walk to school nearby every day, and gaze at the classes from the window with awe and in wonder. She would do this each day since she had an ambition to be educated. Women empowerment is about making sure that she is able to take classes and reach her goals instead of not letting her dream fade or fade away.

"I do not have freedom, but women are unfree regardless of whether her shackles differ to mine." -Audre Lorde

Women's empowerment takes place at the simplest of ways. It doesn't overlook those who are deeply rooted in an unrecognized society. For a small selection of the many empowerment stories Here's a quote by Sarah Omega who had to endure the pain of Obstetric fistula because of the oppression and abuse she endured;

"...if we focus on only treatment , this puts us in the position of having to do it for the rest of our lives. Prevention measures must be put in consideration as the most effective method to reduce maternal morbidity and mortality. Prevention is more than strengthening health systems. It is important to tackle issues like increasing awareness of the importance of the girl-childand strengthening women's self-esteem, self-image and social standing. We must be the first to empower women economically and socially as they are fundamental factors that contribute to the morbidity and mortality of mothers."

Obstetric fistula can be described as a medical condition that is prevalent in the majority of developing nations. It is a complication resulting due to childbirth, which leaves women unable to control her facial or urine. What causes it is a traumatic tale. Obstetric fistula is that is common among young women who get married early and need to bear children at a very high risk age. The same society that brings to this type of circumstance turns its back those who suffer from the condition. The story of Sarah is quite difficult as she was afflicted as a result of rape, and lost her child . In her words;

"Triple punishment! The rape, the loss of my child, and then the leak of urine. At home, my life was miserable. Every night, as my bed got wet from the urine that came out of my body, my pillow became wet from tears resulting from the pain caused by sores on the genital area. While many young people greeted each day with enthusiasm and hopes, to me, every day brought the burden of rejection, humiliation and pain."

The importance of one woman as the pathway to growth or devastation based on the society does to Marie's choice to become an example and a source of inspiration to other young girls in her local community. Marie has a dream to be a woman of her generation and have an impact on her community , and the other girls.

Chapter 4: The Reason We Need Women's Empowerment In Every Way

Today, empower women and empower the entire society.

However absurd it may be, the question of "why women empowerment is important are being asked.

It's not only something that is natural but it's essential. Why not shed some understanding of why women's empowerment shouldn't just be ideas, motions, debates and talks, but put into practice.

Peace

There are a variety of strategies and goals established for achieving world peace. It's a subject of each UN gathering. It does raise the question: how do you get world peace without women and men?' Traditional or patriarchal men may find it absurd to think that women should have to be involved in something as broad as peace in the world. It will be fascinating to learn that the speed of work can't be maintained without women who are strong enough to be an important component that drives.

Have you ever been through long periods of peace? It is likely that a woman was part of the discussions. It's not about being kind. Women naturally think about all possibilities and decide on the most effective solution.

This, if nothing else can be considered a good indicator that women need to be involved in more roles of decision-making.

Women also have an unique ability to connect people which is goldmine.

You can't hear war and peace without the connection of money. One of the most significant benefits to women's jobs is the increasing economic growth. A rise in the financial condition of any country is crucial in making predictions and avoiding war.

What else can womb empowerment do to help to promote peace? You may be asking yourself. An extremely literal way to look at it is the part that women play in the raising of the children who comprise the future generation. If women are empowered, they are able to demonstrate the same empowerment within their homes and provide the proper environment for their children's health development both mentally and physically.

The instincts of women are often on the right path and women are more likely to be aware of any conflict within the community, whether moderate or extremely high. Women are at the front of any disruption or conflict in the social sphere and are prone to the negative effects of conflict.

With these great instincts can come better chances to be at peace.

Societal development

"Women's liberties are the symbol of social liberty." Rosa Luxemburg

In every aspect of industry and business can continue to contribute to its advancement. Women are crucial and essential for the advancement of any field. In the present, women have played key roles in a variety of areas like engineering, medicine, science and military, government and business, education, and so on. Their participation in these fields has had an impact, and has led to a clear development.

Economic development

Dare I say that women empowerment and economic development are two different sides of one coin. While the development process will result in women's empowerment, empowerment of women can also bring about advancement. Both are in sync with the progress of the entire world. To clarify, the concept of economic growth that leads to women's empowerment is easy and straightforward. As a nation develops economically as well as in other areas it brings about an environment of modernity, consciousness, an advanced atmosphere and room for women to participate and alter a few things.

It's not a surprise that poverty and literacy go hand in hand. Ignorance and illiteracy are similar birds. In this regard, ignorance is the main reason for gender inequity and a lack access to opportunities and opportunities that women have. When the wealth and economics of a nation and prosperity, it will raise the level of ignorance that surrounds it.

Women are deeply interested in the welfare of their families. They have been known to donate 90 percent of their resources and income to their families.

These types of thinking suggestions can be applied on a massive scale society, when women are provided by the possibility of making an impact.

End poverty and the cycle of an education that isn't being completed.

What you do, you will beget. Empowering female children starts at the simplest stage, which is education. Education for girls is something that cannot be overemphasized. It is the basis and determination of a lot of social issues. If education is not provided to girls, then society suffers the hit. Perhaps the time that it takes for the aftermath to take place is what causes people to forget how important it is for a girl's educational experience.

Women are an integral part of the world. on the planet and play a significant part in the birth of the next generation and shaping the persona they will become. If her education level is declining and so is the education and knowledge for her son, regardless of whether it is woman or a man. A woman who is not educated will most likely have an illiterate or uninformed child. It's an endless and endless cycle of illiteracy and ignorance.

With such high levels of illiteracy, it's difficult to break free from the poverty shackles. From one woman who is denied education comes an era of massive illiteracy, poverty and ignorance just a few being able to break free from this vicious cycle.

Simply put it is impossible for a nation to grow from its insular state without a focus at the child of the woman.

Elimination of discrimination based on gender

The United Nations defines a human right as "rights which are fundamental to all human beings no matter what race, gender or nationality, religious belief, ethnicity, language or any other distinction. Rights of the human person include live and liberty as well as freedom from the torture and slavery freedom of speech and expression and rights to employment, education, and so on. Every person is entitled to these rights without discrimination."

In this way it is evident that both genders have the right to these rights.

Women must have access to education, health, and job opportunities in the same way as men. I didn't use the word "granted" since it is their fundamental right, which, although it is not acknowledged, was and is still being struggled for.

Women's empowerment is crucial to making a lasting and durable change in the world. Eliminating discrimination based on gender will enhance the rights of individuals and decrease physical or emotional violence due to gender. This, in turn, will enhance the wellbeing of everyone and will be beneficial to social advancement.

Security

"I increase my voice, not so that I shout, but to ensure that those who don't have an opinion are heard. ... The truth is that you will not be successful if we are all kept back." Malala Yousafzai

Don't get enough of the "protect women" campaign and the "keep your daughters and wives secure' campaigns, or the "it's not safe for you to go out there' mantras.

Every day, it is claimed that women should be protected from the males and taken care of. It's a fact that human beings have a dark side in them that takes control of them and causes them to commit violent actions. Women are frequently the victim of these grotesque or violent acts due to their vulnerability and body fragility. The most important question each woman and man on the streets should ask themselves is why this be the case?

Be honest and think about it your thoughts loudly to yourself. What is the reason women are required to become vulnerable, dependent and dependent upon others to survive What is the reason women are required to make unnecessary decisions to safeguard themselves against unavoidable disasters?

The only way to stop the threat to women's lives as well as their security will be for those that cause harm women's lives as well as their comforts unsecure. We're suggesting that you empower a woman now and see how she doesn't just defend herself, but also plans a way to stop these infringements against her. Women shouldn't depend on the males of their gender to safeguard themselves. What they require is an accomplice who can work together to eliminate those with a sexist motive.

Not only can women with power intimidate any threat, but she will also render women inaccessible to these threats, rendering them unrecognizable.

A scenario that is in line with this notion is a future-oriented society in which the law acknowledges and recognizes women's right as well as where women are involved in all aspects of government and work. In this kind of society it is difficult for anyone to even contemplate violating a woman's rights because of the consequences which could follow.

To provide a more realistic an example, our ideal town would be named Kingston town. It has five judges, which the majority of them are females. Its police department is a majority female force, and many women have been hired to work in litigation and other top positions in the world of business and government have been filled by approximately 50% women. In a town like this it is impossible to hold negative, or even vile, thoughts about women, to the point of taking them to the ring.

So, I am firmly defending my belief that empowerment of women is the best method to reduce the anxiety around her.

Facilitate progress and change

Knowledge that is untapped is available everywhere. when you draw conclusions from one angle and neglect the other side, you've made a an unsatisfactory attempt at advancement.

A woman is an pool of knowledge that is not fully explored. It's likely that women who are the least basic are very skilled in one area or another. Women are generally emotionally skilled and are attuned to the things that a typical male doesn't notice. Involving women in the process of achieving their rights to inclusion will result in new talents and new ideas that can help bring about changes, create a more robust more inclusive and inclusive culture, boost productivity in all areas of society, and many more. If you had a woman on your group, you'd be able to go through the many doors that you thought wouldn't open and she'd perform it in the correct and correct way, with the wits and wisdom.

Stop Adversities

"hell has no fury like a woman who has been spit on"

The human race is often portrayed as vindictive animals. The need to be powerful is a normal characteristic of all of us however, when there isn't enough the desire for power, something bitter happens. In a world that has two genders who seek power, there is only one gender that is able to take care of the majority of the power. Another gender however is severely lacking in it and resorts to a different method to show their strength or rage.

Without trying to bore you, I will detail this idea more in depth. Men have gained and retained the most power and now we have women with little to no power. When she is afflicted with such bitterness due to the injustices in society and resentment, she turns to other ways to demonstrate her point or express her frustration.

They can lead to accidents, trauma or even a catastrophe. To prevent an outburst, riot or even internal violence from spreading rapidly through the society, it is imperative to empower women and incorporate them in every aspect of the social welfare.

A touching reminder of the importance of women's empowerment in all cultures is in the words of Ruchi 17, a 17-year-old girl from India. In her words;

"Only the girl is at the victim of all the issues that arise from a marriage with a young couple. While many would understand I'd be the one to suffer the burden of all the problems for the rest of my life. Therefore, I took a stand in protest."

Ruchi knew that it was her responsibility for her to stand up and change her ways.

Women's empowerment is extremely important around the globe and offers numerous benefits however it all comes down to the common sense, empathy and the human right. If we don't, we'll all go out of our ways.

Chapter 5: Empowering Women

Although it might be, there are people who have been asking what the purpose of empowering women is?

It's not clear when women's were empowered. The reason for this is that the desire to become empowered to to overcome any kind of oppression is present in all human beings. Therefore, it could have been a starting point from the very beginning.

Based on Hadley Wood, the notion of self-determination and empowerment was widespread after the war. According to her, wives' husbands were taken to war for long time periods, and some would never return. The woman would be left to carry out all the husband's duties in his place. This is most likely to result in an impression of independence that can be handed to the next generation.

Maybe you're wondering if the title Agno dice is similar to yours. If not, I'll let you know that she was, without any absurdity or misrepresentation of facts the first female Gynecologist. The practice of medicine as a woman in a period when this kind of job was not available for women to the extent of death sentences is nothing less than brave and courageous. She was also kind.

This was around 400 BC Another great brain is Rosalind Franklin. Franklin was a chemist who, through her brave actions, she smoothed the process of discovering of DNA's double-helix design.

A not-so recent movement to empower women was initiated by a black woman referred to by the name of Angela Davis. Through her, it was not only to fight for women, but she was fighting to protect the rights of every color citizen in America. She was an outstanding political activist, and played major parts in protests. To this day, she continues to stand for human rights as an defender and an inspiration.

The efforts that are carried out by Vandana Shiva in India are also a remarkable and inspiring movement. Through her diversity, food and water initiatives, she has empowered many women from her community, which has enabled them to sustain their standard of living.

One of my top empowering stories is about Malala Yousafzai, a girl from Pakistan. There is no word that can adequately describe the bravery Malala was. What she did after her death is a amazing story. She wrote a book called "I am Malala," which detailed her struggle to ensure that she's on track with her studies. With great results, she decided to create a foundation which provides education for children and assists students achieve their education rights all over the world. It is the Malala Fund is a great way to improve the lives of the people it has touched and has yet to reach.

You may be thinking about why you went on this journey through history however I'm pretty sure that it wasn't an enjoyable one. The purpose of this story is to prove that women's empowerment is a constant stream of action to guarantee women rights.

The past was a time when all kinds of traditional tactics like protest, money and so on were used to help one society or another.

What can be utilized in today's time and.

Education

In order to begin empowering women on a basic stage is to make sure that she can access all levels of education like the male child.

A woman with a solid education would be free from the burdens of ignorance and would be capable of making informed decisions about both her personal and professional future.

Education can influence the behavior of girls and attitudes just like absence of it could affect her in a negative way.

Job Opportunities

It's not enough to provide a girl with a good education and deny her the opportunity to use her skills and talents. Women in our time and age do not have the same opportunities for job opportunities like their male counterparts. It's still uncommon to see female pilots, engineers, or business owners. It's a male-dominated world it is said. Perhaps, more inclusion in the professional standards would boost the number of women working in these fields, and help to increase women's participation within the society.

Mentoring and orientation

Employment isn't the only way that women can be empowered. There are many different areas that can be utilized in addition to the traditional educational system that can help enable women. The most important thing in women's empowerment, is educate the female child at the ground and make sure that she's conscious of the rights she has and her choices. It is equally important to help her navigate the right path she should decide to follow to be confident and successful within her own society. Women empowerment doesn't just mean being a leader and earning money. It's about creating an optimistic and confident mental attitude in the minds of each female girl or woman.

Invest in women

Some people already know the things they're created to accomplish and how they'd like to do in life, while others require guidance about the many paths they could choose to take. However, it's evident that not all people are fortunate enough to have the support they need to reach their goals or goals whether it's physically or financially.

Women can gain confidence to be more creative by investing in ideas, ideas, inventions as well as their philosophies and goals.

Investing is a practical process by either providing the investors to access funds and the ability to achieve their goals or by encouraging them by cheering them on and making sure that they do not fall down or doubt themselves.

Protest against discrimination

Protests don't have to be violent or aggressive. They may be calm and peaceful. It's simply taking act to stop unfair treatment of certain groups of people.

Protests, in this instance could be expressed in courts, strikes and even protests that are peaceful, depending on the severity of the prejudice is. The lack of pay, the limited resources and harassment of sexual nature is an unavoidable experience that women face at their workplace because of their female gender. The reasons that cause these inhumane acts must be tracked and controlled in order so that women can discover their potential and reach their full potential.

Giving women decision making roles

In recognition of the fact that a lot of women are now in high-ranking places and have decision-making roles throughout the world and in various areas, there's the need to conquer a major hurdle in the field of women's empowerment.

Women who hold these posts can attest to the prejudice they endure as well as the stigma they carry towards women in these positions. Still, there is a lack of understanding and a lack of respect for women who are in positions of power.

The way to overcome this issue is not to retrace your steps instead, but to move forward. With more women achieving top positions and crucial career opportunities for community, this will bring about respect and appreciation of the efforts of women from all over the world.

Encourage entrepreneurship and the acquisition of skills

In its literal sense, empowerment is ensuring that a person is in control of their own life. When you think about the ideal approach to empower women is to empower women to empower themselves. Get involved in the business world or learn the skills.

Women can be empowered by guiding her to become an business owner. You can help her learn how to run a business, and accept the role of an apprentice to assist in learning and training and assist them in developing their career.

Use your voice

With the myriad of ways to help women become empowered it is advisable to make use of our words, in writing or verbally to not just support the actions that are necessary to ensure women's empowerment but also be adamant about any actions that hinder it.

Oprah Winfrey uses her show on broadcast to help women to develop and flourish. She makes use of her voice on her show to address the issues of women.

Chimamanda Adiche is well-known novelist whose writings are loved by a lot of young people across the globe. Her writing is used to address the difficulties faced by women and how they can conquer these challenges.

But, using your voice doesn't require you to be famous and/or an author. Simply speaking about the women around you who may be struggling emotionally or physically.

It's about speaking out about the shameful actions against women and help women break through the barriers that hold women back.

You can use your voice in your everyday conversations, on your social media, and in your thoughts.

Women's empowerment is an outstanding act of justice and equality. It is active, progressive and altering how women live their lives across the globe every day.

Women empowerment is an adventure to change the world. You can be sure of it. It's not to be aggressive, but in spite of the advancements in technology in our modern age but the prevailing thoughts of our minds is still outdated. This is evident by the prevalence of classism, racism religion-based disputes, as well as gender discrimination.

Women empowerment can be a method to prevent society from falling deep into other forms discrimination. In an environment where women aren't discriminated against and instead are recognized and respected, it will only require just a bit more effort to end discrimination based on race and inequality of class.

When we talk about women's empowerment, it's not just about gender bias. It is directed towards the plight of the poor and illiterate that plagues all over the world. Women's empowerment is a way to combat poverty, inequality and climate change, as well as social inequality, and injustice.

The empowerment of women can also improve the overall health and well-being of women across the globe. We spoke about Sarah Omega and her ordeal with the obstetric fistula. With the help of knowledge and support from society stories such as hers will be gone forever and we will be more healthy women, and, in turn, the next generation with a healthy one.

A new future for women

The future is female. More women are born in the modern world. Statistics on population will reveal that women are more prevalent than males. It's not good for anyone to have a large number of women who are helpless and without empowerment. It is beneficial for all of humanity to have women equipped and strong enough to face any challenge that may are presented.

It's pretty straightforward. When a kingdom is in decline and male soldiers are drastically reduced it is only when the king realize that his female subjects can take the sword and fight well. But wouldn't it be too late since they weren't giving sticks to practice with before those of their male counterparts? In investing in women, you are making a bet for the future. We all fight to survive and excluding the vast resources of women due to the desire to be a hero or an act of ignorance.

The Viking women of the past were known to train and eventually become shield maidens. They were able to fight with ferocity in wars, and even become warriors. Their ability to work with females made possible the victory in the Vikings and many of their victories.

The land they inherited was not vulnerable simply because they had left women in the dust. Women of any age could opt to become a warrior, and an unflinching one at the same time.

Applying this tale to our current day and age means forming a front to combat inequality, climate change and poverty, illiteracy and underdevelopment in all its forms and in all regions of the globe.

Women empowering women

Women, it's our duty to encourage the empowerment of other women.

The reason we are empowered is to be free from the chains of patriarchal system. The males may hold a sway on the power of world however, as women we're capable of overcoming every obstacle.

It is essential to share our voices, encouragement and actions to help women around us and helping them succeed in their goals and dreams.

Women should not be overlooked and they can bring about significant changes and growth.

It is important for women to establish foundations, like the one Malala Yousafzai started. You have a responsibility to inspire women in your circle and help women achieve their goals. You'll require their strength and numbers.

The aim is to rule the world by empowering yourself.

Make sure you voice your opinion across all your social media platforms. Declare loudly and clearly that women are going to change the world in a significant way.

Chapter 6: It's Yours Too Can Do It!

In this section, I'd like to tell you the true stories of several women that have come up from the lowest. One of my top model women, J.K Rowling is surely at the top of the list.

Joanne Kathleen Rowling

To me, she is an example of what a woman can do to influence the world with the arts. While financial contributions are not the only thing she has made her work has been a source of inspiration for many people in the world, female and male alike.

She was the one who brought to life an iconic and adored characters ever created: Harry Potter! Harry Potter is loved and loved by all kinds of categories as well as nations, cultures and cultures alike. Amazingly, J.k Rowling went through many difficulties before she could publish her Harry Potter books!

Today, J.K Rowling is not just one of the top female writers but she is also one of the few female authors to be billionaire. She has inspired many youngsters to imagine and many writers in their writing, and provided us with an insight into the mysterious world of Hogwarts. What's not to love about this incredible woman? please!

Oprah Winfrey

In the realm of powerful females who made a a mark in the world, no one is more influential than Oprah Winfrey!

She has been through the tough streets of not just gender discrimination , but racial discrimination too. She has been able to overcome every obstacle and has not backed down or given up. She is now one of the most influential women in the media and has greatly contributed to the advancement of the world, women's empowerment and the rights of women.

She has inspired a lot of people and remains as a significant source of inspiration. It is important to know that she began her TV career when she was an teen and then went on becoming the youngest only African-American woman to be able to read the headline news on a television station located in Nashville, America at the young age of 19! Do you think about that?

Her popularity exploded in 1986 thanks to The Oprah Winfrey Show, which was a huge success for the next twenty-five years. She then went one step further and established her own television channel, The Oprah Winfrey Network.

She is now one of the most well-known, popular, and well-loved interviewers. Also, she has been backed by a majority of Americans to contest the American president's seat!

Coco Chanel

When we talk about women and fashion, we discuss it in a different way. When we discuss fashion we are talking about Coco Chanel. The fashion world wouldn't exist today without the iconic fashion icon Coco Chanel.

The woman's dress, the tiny black dress, and the purse with a quilted design are all inventions of Coco Chanel. Coco Chanel learned sewing from a young age. Her first store opened around 1900 and that was mostly focused on designing the hats. Then, she began to venture into clothes also and, by around 1920, she launched her first fragrance.

Today, nearly 100 years since it was first created, Chanel No 5 is still considered to be one of the most renowned fragrances. It was born from a hat shop , and became become one of the world's most admired and reliable luxury brands worth millions of dollars.

Coco Chanel is a model for many women and men to pick up their sewing machines and create beautiful clothes.

She has embraced her fair portion of charitable giving and helped in the advancement and modernization of the fashion industry around the globe.

Coco Chanel was incredibly concerned about women's empowerment. The majority of her fashion-related innovations were created to free women from the fashion industry. She wanted to allow women their freedom of dressing way they like and wear whatever they want to wear, and prove it was not just about just household management. Her famous fragrance Chanel NO.5 was born out of her desire to define the modern modern woman she embodied.

Mother Teresa

"There aren't any great things, just small things that are accompanied by great love. Happiness is in those who"

Mother Teresa is the embodiment of a woman who is strong, awe-inspiring caring, compassionate smart, and most important, she is a keeper of peace.

She was the first woman to receive canonization at the hands of the Catholic Church on September 4, 2016 in Saint Peter's square, Vatican City by Pope Francis.

She has been a huge contributor to the well-being of numerous poor orphans, sick and dying people and has touched the lives of thousands of lives.

Mother Teresa is known for her selfless sacrifices for the world's less fortunate. Her legacy is an inspiring women around the globe.

Michelle Obama

Ladies Our loved former First Lady of the United States is the first African-- American woman to be elected as the first lady of the United States.

Michelle Obama served as an advocate for awareness of poverty as well as adult and child education as well as physical and nutrition as well as the necessity for healthy food choices.

She is considered an iconic fashion model who is supportive of American designers. She also topped the poll by Gallup in 2020 of the top ladies in America.

She has written books, including American mature and Becoming. Her influence isn't linked to her husband's presidency or her prior FLOTUS position (First Lady in the United States) as is evident.

She has been an inspiration for a lot of women and has inspired a number of women across the globe.

She is actively involved in many charity work across the globe and remains among the most influential and inspiring women of our time.

The women struggled towards their influential podiums. When they did they stuck to their beliefs and allowed their voices to be heard. Because of their unique contribution to the world, they have contributed a lot to the progress of the world.

There are many women who, in some way or the other, contributed to making the world an improved place. The list of them and their contribution to humanity and the world could eliminate the world of its paper since I am sure that you your own self, have in one manner or another helped make the world more beautiful.

Chapter 7: "Know Your Worth"

There are a lot of women are caught up in marrying someone who isn't her standards. We've all witnessed them and a lot of women have responded similarly with the words, "I don't know what she is seeing in him" or "She is better than him." In the majority of cases, women lose much of their income or even their lives, because of the man who did not merit her. You may also see an attractive young woman who is in front of various men who aren't even anywhere near deserving her body, nor her worthiness.

Have you ever wondered why women marry a man far below her standards or even give her body to unworthy men? If not, let me to shine a the light on this mystery for you. The reason women do these things is just because she doesn't understand or appreciate what she's worth.

There's a passage in Proverbs 11:22 which states, "As a ring of gold is in the snout of a swine can be a beautiful woman without discernment." Let's examine this in its most fundamental meaning. A gold-plated ring could be considered to be a gorgeous item of jewellery, isn't it? Based on its thickness and size and thickness, it could be worth a nice penny, surely? Pigs are as one of the most filthy and disgusting creatures in the world. A very filthy animal which would be unable to appreciate for such a gorgeous piece of jewelry such as an earring made of gold. In knowing the value and value of this stunning piece of jewelry Why would you want to take it and place it inside the snout of a pig? What is the reason you would devalue its value and worth in this manner? Why would you, wouldn't you?

Webster's dictionary defines discretion as "the capacity to decide or follow one's own judgment; the virtue of being discrete." This means that we have two approaches to this. Let's begin by having the ability to be discreet.

A woman who doesn't have discretion or has a limited number of choices is the same as the gold ring on the snout of that pig. When she is surrounded by numerous males, she is taking nothing away from her worth and worth. The men who could be classified as pigs because of their actions and conduct, will probably not appreciate her for the stunning and gorgeous woman (certainly with a beautiful gold ring) she is. Their sole purpose would be to play on "the dirt" (their mattress) and then take her out in the world filthy and dirty. After all, once the "pigs" have been able to get her, what would her worth be?

Many young women (and some of the older ones, too) aren't aware of the significance of their body is. They don't realize how their body is temples and a vessel in which life is born and nurtured. The basis that your body has the capacity to support life makes you valuable. Why does an aspiring young woman or girl not know what she is worth? There are a myriad of variables that determine what is worth it but the most important reason is that, well nobody has probably ever given her an exact estimate of the value she's worth.

The father of a young girl is believed to be the very first male who she is taught to love and is the first person to show her how precious and beautiful she truly is. Through this relationship, she discovers not only what it feels and is like to be loved and loved by a male and how she is expected to be loved by one. Women who have enjoyed a loving father/daughter relationship generally have confidence in themselves. However, over the last couple of decades growing numbers of young girls have grown in a world without that bond which means they don't have any idea of how beautiful or valuable they truly are. The first compliment they receive from males usually revolves around the body part they are wearing. Thus they begin to connect their worth to their body. How attractive their breasts appear. How round their butts are. The gorgeousness of their legs. Their beauty is determined by their body , not by their presence as all. They start to draw the attention of young boys by their appearance and not their soul. Then they begin having sexual relations. They begin to hear many other compliments regarding that portion of their.

They lose the complete understanding of how to grab the attention and heart of a man through these characteristics that are in their own, i.e. their passion and sweetness as well as their personality. They are able to win the heart of a man and his attention by virtue of the attributes they have without, i.e. their physiques, their looks and their va-jay-jay.

They don't realise that those attributes they are missing are only superficial. They don't last. They can make her get fatter, shed appearance, or her va-jayjay will wear out and leave her without a solid foundation to base her self-worth upon, she is depressed and unhappy and lacking self-confidence and self-esteem. Once she is at the point of no return, her life is gone, since she'll be laying beneath any man who gives her the affection she longs for. Unaware of her true worth as a person, she offers her preciousness to any pig she likes, or more accurately she adores her.

It is a vicious cycle that begins during the preteen years of a girl's young age and continues until she is in her adulthood. I'm sure that you've been around these girls that were considered to be the most popular during high school. The boys adored their gorgeous face and cute shape. But when the reunion of ten years comes around her appearance isn't as beautiful She's put on around 80 pounds. She has three children by three different males. She's nothing more than a shadow of the woman she used to be. Women who don't remain discreet about the quality of the men they are sleeping with don't know is that every when you offer yourself to a man the man takes a portion of you to him, but you will keep a portion of him as well.

In retrospect the moment young women lay on the floor with a guy who has no respectable character or has any morals about him Not only is he is sapping you of any virtues you have and he's making sure you don't have anything to replenish the ones he's obtained. In fact it's likely that he's left you with something more threatening. Particularly, if he scatters the seeds of his own inside the person you are.

My wish is that you ladies will realize the value of your own self. The redeeming and wonderful characteristics are not just in the outside world but inside you. Your soul, your essence the way you conduct yourself as well as your personality, confidence, and self-esteem; those are the characteristics that make you attractive. These attributes are not affected by age or weight growth. They can only be changed by the person who is. You are the gods of your temples. A man is able to improve your life. He could even help build your confidence. But the foundation needs to be laid before that, and If you don't have a great father or any positive male person in your life to help you lay the base, you have to undertake the job of laying it by yourself.

Stop placing yourself in the mouth of those animals who don't first, know what you really are worth and, two don't want to find out. You are more discerning about whom you let touch your nails and hair than who you will allow to enter your body. That's an unspoken fact. Now is the time to get tighter your muscles your neck, straighten that crown to your face and discover your real identity. When you do this you will help the man in your life understand hisown, as you tell him "Yeah I'm feeling you, but you're in need of to improve your manner of speaking. I'm Queen in every sense and therefore I cannot be seen out as a court jester. Bring yourself together, love." This is the power women have that they do not even know you possess however you aren't able to use it until you realize the person you were before.

Let's move on to the second portion of our definition "the ability to make decisions or follow one's own judgment." I'll be honest in a short time here. I've got plenty of respect and love for women but, honestly many of you women's judgment in deciding to choose men, is not a good one! I'm a male, and I've at times been thinking"to myself, "What is she really thinking?" Not to worry however. Big Brotha Jah will be able help you understand why this issue is present and help you eliminate it. Follow me in this scenario quickly.

Imagine if the top luxury cars, such as Benzes, Bentleys, Lambos, Aston Martins, and any other exotic vehicle could decide the person they wanted they'd like their drivers to be. Imagine that you spot a

Bentley driving down the street with a filthy, dirty crackhead sitting in the driver's seat. The car hasn't been cleaned and the crackhead was able to get the car packed with his friends who are crackheads and they're smoking marijuana in the car, while they are putting their dirty feet out the windows. Your first thought would be what? What is the reason why a stunning and expensive car choose an unappreciative, low-grade owner? It's going to blow your mind, wouldn't it? Now imagine you're seeing the sight of a Porsche on the road. The driver's side mirror hangs down in a broken state and one of the rims is bent from hitting the curb, and the black smoke is streaming out of the exhaust pipe. You then see this jerk driving behind the car, and he's being erratic and crazy and spinning into the middle of the road and driving up and down the sidewalk. What are your first thoughts? Why didn't this stunning machine choose someone who was more responsible, mature and self-controlled?

There are a lot of you who lack judgment look like the luxury cars in that situation. We can tell by the way you dress and what you've got in your life, that you're probably of a particular kind of woman, however, we also see this naive and malicious creature that you've allowed yourself get attached to that is truly mind-blowing. It's true that the opposite attracts, however sometimes it's time to think about the exact nature of what that you're attracting.

I had the pleasure of meeting this girl when I was around 18 years old. She was beautiful. A real sweet, intelligent and soft spoken. She was simply a and down to earth individual. Her upbringing was in a one parent household with parents who loved her. True Forever Girl through and through. However, she was in love and was surrounded by the back of a man who was a complete slob to her. He spoke to her as if she was a stray creature playing in his garbage container or something. He kept cheating on her. He beat her. He just dragged her through the dirt. However, she would always return to him and I was unable to understand why for my life. She picked her own men, but she chose the one who was most destructive and disruptive to her well-being. Like a moth to flame.

I am aware that there are several factors that lead women to be the knucklehead after she's with him, however I'm more concerned with the procedure that occurs before she ever ties herself with him. A lot of women have an unflattering self-esteem that they believe they cannot be better than what they're receiving, or two avoid the warning signs due to the fact that they'd rather be left alone. They've become so deficient in self-esteem that even an idiot with a string attached to a stick could take them down. However, the most sad part about it, that, most of the time this isn't even a fair representation of yourself. Your self-consciousness doesn't allow you to be the person you really are. It's similar to being in the front the one or two fun mirrors in your home and distorted the real picture of yourself.

Most of these men scavengers prefer to not see yourself as the person you really are, since they are aware that you're way far from their realm. So, when they have you, they put the "foot in your neck" take off your gorgeous wings and place you inside an enclosure. This is to ensure that you not be able to fully realize your potential, as they think that if you fail you'll soon recognize their incompetence and lack of significance and leave them immediately. Insecurities, lower self-esteem, and deficiency of self-worth can be an opportunity for them. It's like someone put the wrong price on an Lexus and was able to purchase the Lexus at the cost of an lawnmowers.

This low self-esteem is a result of the fact that you didn't receive it from dad when you were a young girl. As a result, you are constantly searching for a dad and that's why it draws you to a lot the clowns. It's not clear that you are entitled to better. You aren't aware the possibility of finding better. There was no one who said anything about your wings. Therefore, you aren't aware that you're an angel. You were never shown your crown, therefore you aren't aware that you're a queen. Your perception of men's opinions sucks due to your expectations and pictures of yourself are skewed.

This is where the emergence and realization of self-worth is interconnected with the growing in a man's personality. I said in the beginning that men prefer to be around women. They'll pay that ridiculous cover fee at the club in the knowledge that there'll be plenty of women. When women realize that they have earned better and aren't going to take anything less than that What do those guys will need to do if they want to join you? Improve himself. Any man who is truly an exemplary character ought to be looking to make that change. What incentive do an individual have to improve on what the way he's currently doing all the perks and is already an uninvolved lazy slob? The things that we males enjoy is what we'll have the freedom to do it.

Here's more free jewelry to give you. Stop being scared to be on your own. Desperate women make desperate decisions. I'll repeat it. Desperate women make desperate decisions. Being in solitude is a virtue and there's a different between being lonely and lonely. Being alone indicates confidence and self-assurance within yourself. Only women who are desperate to be left alone. women who are desperate lack discretion. The judgment she makes is faulty as the desire to have her loneliness overcome is greater than making a good decision when choosing a partner.

If women spend half the time and energy they invest in deciding on what they will wear to leave for a night out into choosing which man they would offer their bodies and hearts to, you'll instantly eliminate half the b.s. that y'all experience. If you choose one of them, and you find that he's not the best fit with you. Do not be scared or embarrassed to break off connections with the person. It's impossible to tell if a shoe is comfortable for us without trying it on, don't you think? If not, we can simply choose a different pair. The relationship should be easy and simple. You wouldn't want to keep the shoes that weren't fitting because they're cute are you? You're welcome to ignore thatbecause I could hear the whole booming, "Hell yeah's," at this point. Also, scratch that. Poor example. But, you understand what I am trying to convey. The man you choose to marry should complement your personality and blend into your soul and heart effortlessly and effortlessly. If you're trying to force to accept him in your heart to make him feel at home, he's probably not suppose to be in your heart. It's that simple.

Let your wings fly take flight, straighten that crown of your head, and discover what you're really worth, not just to men but to the world as well.

Chapter 8: High Maintenance/High Standards

The word used to describe maintenance is maintain. This is "to assist or ensure the maintenance of." For the woman he adores and cherishes it's a joy for a man. He will be there for your needs, however only within the limits he's capable of. For some women that are not enough. You believe that men's money is superior to his character and beliefs. You don't want to be loved all your life. You desire to be spoilt to the max.

You require an individual who can sustain the maintenance of the life style that you've incorporated yourself. Ladies, I'll tell you that you'll never find the man you want. When I refer to a man I'm talking about the kind of guy who enters the room confidently. The kind of person who gets your pants wet the moment you look at him , because he radiates such gentlemanly traits. The kind of person who earns money and refuses to let money define him. Without or with that money, he's still a man.

The only thing you'll likely ever see is the sucker. A tender-dick. A small boy who happens to have some cash. The kind that was not used to beautiful women giving his attention until he was able to earn money. Don't think I'm being naive, there are plenty of suckas to choose from. However, be aware that you'll never be satisfied and content with the guy. Why is that? Because you realize that you're a sucka, too. You realize that he's ridiculous. That's why you loved the guy and you prayed for him to begin with. Therefore, you can let the gifts as well as the vehicles as well as the clothes and the rest of the things that he might give you to please your needs for a while however, after a few Birkin bags, and shopping trips you'll eventually become repetitive. This is what happens every time.

Once it happens, you'll begin to long for the kind of chemistry and bond that truly makes a relationship unique If you discover that there's no sign of it and he'll lose interest to you. In the meantime, your dildo is likely to satisfy your sexual desires more than his partner will.

A majority of women will at some point when they're interested in guys, will seek out the man whom they feel "does that" to them. The man whose sound of his voice can make her unique parts thump throughout the night. The sum of money you spend will never buy that kind of feeling. And as you get older, but never getting this sensation from the guy (or men) whom you're in a relationship with, these alliances will begin to look like an unrealized relationship. You'll be very unhappy inside And no amount of money you spend on him can ease the discontent, or fill the gap.

Some women are so shallow that a friendships can be sufficient to keep them going. However, these types of women don't require lots of things to fill their souls with nourishment, since regardless of the reason, they're hollow. They're like the chocolate Easter bunnies I mentioned you receive at Easter that look great and attractive in the outer appearance, yet once you bite into them you find it hollow and empty in the middle.

But, ladies, you remain like the other chocolate bunny I loved, which appears pretty and appealing in the outer appearance, but the moment you bite it there's nothing but chocolate through it, this kind of superficial and hollow relationship won't keep your soul nourished or nourished. If women of this type is prone to becoming shallow is usually due to one or two reasons: (1) she has also suffered trauma and is unwilling to be a part of the relationship and (2) they were taught to behave as the one above.

The truth is out there about this. Women do not emerge from the womb like gold-diggers. It's an acquired and learned characteristic that behaviour and thought tends to be put in the context of covering up some painful experience. If I come across women who put the pursuit of money ahead of the love for love I often consider, "I wonder what she's scared of?" Now, don't be fooled, I think that a woman ought to have a confidence in herself. If you're certain that you're an Ferrari it is true that you should not let a man treat you as an ordinary dirt bike. What I'm referring to here is making someone pay you for the privilege of being an authentic Ferrari. You've made your self-worth more valuable and sold it to the most expensive bidder. When that man appears and treats you like a piece property, you feel your emotions.

Make sure you know this; ALL men, even the suckas and tricks recognize when they're being manipulated. However, most of them aren't concerned so long as they get what they want from the deal, while they're the majority who refuse to acknowledge that they're being used. They prefer to play with the idea of you enjoying them as they're playing with in their minds. These men who are desperate are the ones you should will really delve into and put it on the thick. If that's what you're looking for in a guy in an intimate relationship, then be what you can to be the best. Try to be maximum abilities. Don't be sour or begin to complain about the things you've gone through because of being this way. Accept everything in the way it is. Dress in your big girl pants and fade whatever might result out of it. I'm sure you'll appreciate this. This book isn't meant designed for people like you. However, if you're someone who happens to be living this way and, behind closed doors you're crying and wishing you could find a guy who would love you unconditionally for who you are or looking for a more satisfying kind of love relationship it's you who I'm sending this book to. You are who you are.

You're probably admired by your girls at home due to how you interact with men and the presents you receive however, as quiet as it is and you're jealous of those women who stay at home with their families. You feel a tingle of jealousy when you observe couples out and about enjoying each and observe women shining and radiant not because of the latest pair of designer shoes as well as Chanel diamond earrings that they've received, but rather from the affection, love, and affection they receive each day from the men who appreciate and admire them for who they are. If you try to sabotage this kind of connection, claiming that you don't really need it, you're deceiving (and doing a prank on) nobody else but yourself.

Take off the façade to admit you're afraid to death of having to be vulnerable and open to the man of your dreams. After you've made that first step, you'll be instantly strongerbecause you've identified and acknowledged what's true. It's impossible to resolve an issue in the event that you don't think it exists at all. It is impossible to repair a wound if aren't willing to acknowledge you're injured. You can fool yourself into thinking that things like material possessions will satisfy your soul and then you'll have a life that isn't fulfilled. I've already mentioned this within the text. It's acceptable to inform a man that you've been hurt or you're afraid. Many men want to play the role of knight-in-silver for the damsel in need. First, you have to allow him the chance to become the one.

Stop being a timid little girlwho hides in expensive shoes, clothes and purses. While you're dazzling our eyes with diamonds also blinded by your own fears and pain. Being the most lavish is a lie that you make up to conceal what's actually there. It's your carapace , which you slide away to keep yourself from the challenges and disappointments in relationships.

Let's turn our focus on your cousin. The one with highest standards. I have to approach this slightly more cautiously since I don't intend to appear as if I'm somehow advocating for males who do not put forth an effort worthy of being an honest man. I believe that setting the highest standards for what you expect for a man is advantageous and intelligent, but certain people go overboard with it. That is something I'd like to discuss.

It is believed that the higher an individual woman is on the financial or corporate ladder and the higher up she climbs, the more difficult it is to find a compatible partner. This is due to a reason that's double-edged. When women ascend the ladder her expectations and standards of men will also increase along with her. The higher she rises the higher the expectations usually rise too. As the air becomes thinner the further you climb toward the sky and the fewer the number of males gets when you reach that tax bracket. This issue is more than doubled when you're a woman of ethnicity. In addition, when you move up the step and into the tax bracket you're with men on the same ladder. But, remember this: as men climb this step and the tax bracket they can shed certain characteristics women might admire in a man. For example the humility.

The men who are the most successful climb up in their status, and often their egos grow with it. They are more likely to become aggressive, narcissistic and irritable. They're more interested in their own happiness than on yours. However, this isn't 100. Yes, men who have wealth or status don't have these traits, however in the selection pool which women are required to select from, the odds of encountering a man who has those undesirable traits are much higher.

Therefore, looking back, ladies, you might not meet a man with the traits you admire or admire within your tax bracket. this is when these high standards could become a hassle. You start to think that "Girl There aren't any decent men in this world," and, relating to the of men it could be true in your opinion. Buton a bigger scale, this claim is a complete sham. I know that women of a certain type and height would like to find a man who is a bit confident, for example ambition, ambition, or financial security however it is important to understand that men can possess all these qualities but maybe on an entirely different degree.

He may not earn 70-100k a year driving a Benz or being an executive in an Fortune 500 company, but you could make 40K-50K annually and driving a luxurious truck and working for an organization he's worked working for ten to more than twenty years. He owns his own home expenses, has a job, and is pretty good for himself. However, this gentleman is likely to be overlooked since his achievements don't meet your expectations. Many people are ambitious to the max and haven't capable of getting over that hurdle or make the proper connections to connect it all. Don't let that affect the personality of this man, however.

My wife constantly tells me how she's fortunate to be able to have me in the world, however I remind her the fact that this isn't luck. She went outside the comfort zones and did something that she never ever thought of doing in her life: write to a man in prison. However, through her rather than lowering her standards, and by bending her expectations a little and letting her standards be a bit softer, she was able to meet who is now not just her husband but also her most trusted friend and partner as well. Of course, this story isn't for everyone however, there are many similar stories that are waiting to be told in the event that a large number of women followed their heart instead of their standards.

Ladies, your gut can be a gift granted to you by God will let you know whether a person is right to you, or not. You'll receive this affirmation from your soul and not in your va-jay-jay. However, you have to be willing to receive the possibility of receiving it. If you're able to speak up attending an event like a Black Tie occasion or another event where you believe you have that a certain type of man will attend and you're not allowed to go to the supermarket, the gas station, or even at the mall due to the fact that the kind of man you're looking for won't be there You're doing yourself, and perhaps your heart, a huge injustice. This is the truth that's not spoken about. You do not know which part of the world God has placed your husband or hidden away. You don't know where God has your partner in life and Your Anam Cara (Google for it) put in. God isn't always going to wrap your husband and your life partner with gold trimmings or a red bow tied on his head. Your ideal husband could be a few feet behind you at the supermarket or waiting next to you at the barbecue place.

Also, remember that good men can be found in all sizes, shapes, shades in tax brackets and shapes. My grandfathers from the two sides of my lineage not rich, but honest men. Therefore, my grandmothers were by their side until their deaths and never got married to any other man after their deaths. They didn't have expensive automobiles, or had the money to place my grandmother in the most expensive mansions however, they cared for their family and loved ones without any complaint or grumble. My grandmothers loved them until the end of time. A lot of women with these standards place too the emphasis on what a man has or creates, instead of the character traits that he displays, the values of his family and the values that he adheres to as man. If you start to judge a man based on his 401(K) and his car or bank accounts, and the suits he is wearing without thinking about it, you've eliminated the real man.

Let's look at the opposite side of this quality coin, for one moment. We'll look at the women who set their standards on male's physical characteristics. He must be at minimum 6'2" and have a thigh full of muscles, dark-skinned and at least 8 inches of space between the legs (calm your little hot tails down. I'm trying to get across the point here.) It isn't a problem if he beats you every day and verbally abuses your? Is it okay if he's no morals, and is sleeping with your cousin and your best friend? What if he's an unrepentant father? It's fine, but is it? Do you recognize how weak your standards become when you base them entirely on physical characteristics?

The real essence and value of a woman or man and gentlemen, lies within his own self, not in him. It's not possible to place a crown on clowns and call them a King. If all you're seeking is a guy with an elegant car and a large ding-dong, it's a shame to admit it, but you're not expecting anything. Your expectations might have fallen short of what you think they were. That means that anyone with an exotic car and a good piece of meat will knock you off your feet.

Let me talk to you about something about my own snobbish standards I used to have at some point. I've never had an unisexual relationship as I was an adult. I'd never been engaged to a relationship. However, as I began to improve my self-esteem and my character I longed to be a husband. Not just an ordinary spouse, but also a great husband. Despite the circumstances I was determined to be a great man to a woman, and so I started to ask God to bless me with an ideal woman. I informed Him that I knew I've hurt a lot of women throughout my life however, If He could just be gracious to me again I promised to be a good man to her.

As I am a Black male, I am in love with my ladies. Never had I dated anyone other than in recent times, I've been saying, "I don't care if she's blue, as long as she's a decent woman I'll go with her." While I had made this statement, I never imagined myself as anything other than one Black woman. It's true that God has a sense humor, and He will force you to stick to your promises and prayer. When I say that my wife happens be a first-generation Swedish American, but to society's eyes, she's an White woman. When I first met her, I said to that she, "I never thought that I'd see an White woman in front of me" and I was referring to that. My wife is so much more than an wife. She has also become a long-term acquaintance. I have learned many things about myself and life generally. But, I need to consider, what if I thought the standards I set for myself were low that I'd stated, "I ain't talking to anyone who is a White women." I could have been unable to enjoy an amazing and enjoyable experience. In reality, the color of her skin isn't important to me. What I can see are beautiful woman who I know is available in all hues and ethnicities. What I see is my closest friend, whom I can twitch in one moment and then have an intense philosophical conversation the next. What I can see now is a person who was adamant about me, despite my flaws and imperfections. I see a woman who has patience with me. She inspires me and inspires me to smile. That pushes me to become better than I was. I do not think of any White woman, I find a woman that is kind, compassionate, and funny, and has the most beautiful of spirits. It's that simple and that's it.

The following excerpt from James Allen's book The Eight Pillars of Prosperity summarizes the issue very well: "By clinging to stubborn beliefs, what pleasures are lost, which friends are sacrificed, what joy is lost and what future prospects are destroyed!"

My point is that we don't get our blessings often times due to our personal excessive (and often shallow) standards. The majority of women are looking for to have a financially stable and handsome guy who will get her toes curled and then blow her out all at once. Also, she wants a guy who can bring her laughter, make her feel safe, beautiful and special. She is looking for a man who whom she will admire and take lessons from. It is possible to achieve this however, you might have to compromise your own standards in order to find him.

He could be driving the Honda instead of an BMW. He could be working in construction instead of working in the corner office. He might not be a typical beauty, but he has an incredibly beautiful heart. He may also be in jail instead of an apartment in a penthouse. If you are in agreement with them and/or not facts are the truth. Sometimes, we pray and ask God to grant us things however God is capable of realizing how much you truly want that particular thing. What would you give up for love and happiness?

Would you give up the ability to get the latest purse each month, if he made you feel gorgeous every day? Would you give up your pride and let that gentleman to take you home in the back of a Ford instead of a Cadillac and be sure that you'll enjoy the best most enjoyable time with him? Would you be willing to sacrifice him not having the ability to travel with you to exotic destinations when you felt like you were the best in the world? Would you be willing to sacrifice an ethnicity different to yours when you knew it was him you've been dreaming of since forever?

It's like playing a game of chess which is why sometimes you need to examine this game a bit more deeply to determine the best move to take to achieve what you want to achieve. If it's love that you're really trying to achieve, take a examine a bit more deeply the maninstead of simply skimming over the surface. Diamonds, gold as well as oil are submerged in mud, stones and dirt. I made that statement to emphasize that the most beautiful and valuable things in the world are most often concealed in the least desirable locations or in the most dangerous situations. Find out how to view the person with your heart, not by your standards. Whatever he might lack in material but does he compensate for it in a spiritual way? Whatever he might not have physically, can she succeed in her mind?

It's about time to look at ourselves before we are too quick to put the blame on others. Because of social pressures, we tend to position ourselves to be not being shallow, materialistic or racist, but the reality is that a majority of the time, our values and biased choices do not reflect that. Therefore, you should re-examine them and consider what your own standards really reflect about you as a person and for an individual woman. Love is all-encompassing when you let it be.

Chapter 9: Ms. Indivisible (The Alpha Female)

We've all met this woman. She owns her house. She owns her own vehicle. It pays for her own expenses. One of her favorite things she's quick to say is "I do not need a man." So the woman will usually have an assortment of sex toys to meet the "needs." The woman refers to the Rabbit the man she has become. She's extremely assertive and confident, as well as self-confident and confident. She's goal-oriented and career-driven, as well as determined. The idea of becoming an ordinary housewife freaks her out in a huge way.

I'm going to add an exclamation point in this article before I proceed. I am awestruck by these kinds of women for having taken on the challenge after a man in their lives probably fell off the bat. They've done whatever it takes to ensure their lives are successful and stable, as well as positive and productive. However, when they've assumed the man's role which means taking home the bacon and putting on pants at the house, they've forgotten certain traits that women are supposed to have. She's not sure how to behave towards her husband in the absence of bedroom (and occasionally inside the bedroom as well). She doesn't make big decisions to anyone other than her, because she's come to rely and trust her own judgments. Some women don't have children because they fear they'll ruin their careers.

Also, I congratulate the women who have figured out ways to succeed in a male-dominated society however, this book is about finding true love, and I'm going to address the proportions (no regardless of how tiny it might be) of career-driven independent women who are wondering why they are unable to find the right partner. This is the truth that's not spoken about. The majority of these types of women would like men, but they are often the cause of their own mistakes in things that matter to the heart. Here's why.

The majority of us are aware of that an "Alpha Male" is. He's a confident, dominant and over-achieving person who believes in his self-confidence with complete confidence. Alpha Males are typically aggressive, territorial and possess the traits of an effective leader. Most Alpha Males don't like to be challenged.

Many women who have assumed this role of independence have acquired the traits and characteristics that are characteristic of an Alpha Male and have created the new type of woman known as the Alpha Female. While this is an desirable position for women but it's not the normal course of life. And that is where things tend to be a little hazy.

If an Alpha female goes into the dating world it's because she's walking out as two distinct women: one who is natural and the other not. The normal woman desires to be nurtured and loved she is caring and loving and follows her husband's instructions. The Alpha Female however generally is the one who is the main provider the most, and is the one who follows her own rules. Therefore, if she comes upon a person who is the Alpha male, they will usually meet up in the process because that Alpha Female inside her will not be a quiet person. So, you'll find two dominant personalities vying for the top spot because it's unlikely to be simple for the Alpha Female to suddenly assume a backseat position. She's used to being the leader and will confront him in some way regardless of whether it's completely unintentionally.

Women who have navigated their vessel through a variety of dangerous storms and uncharted waters, and managed to get through it all is not likely to surrender steering wheel as quickly, and an Alpha Male is looking to control the wheel. This is the time when the scenario in which a man complains that his wife is "too controllable." The man will think that she is seeking to turn him into the head of the relationship, and instead of the brain. It all depends on the kind of personality a man is, this kind of relationship could turn ugly. An ignorant Alpha Male tends to be violent when confronted. In his head the goal is to destroy her spirit and reduce her to an echelon. He's determined to knock this Alpha so that she will never be able to challenge him ever again. These Alpha

Males with self-discipline and values will leave after she continued to push him. He's a leader and if she doesn't give him the chance to lead, he'll locate someone else who can.

Another option to solve this issue is for Alpha/Independent Females to meet someone who has a personality type B. People with this kind are silent, quiet and aloof to others. They aren't typically leaders, nor do they try to take control of the steering wheel. They tend to "go by the flow" sort of mentality. For the Alpha females, that might be the ideal man but it is important to remember that the different woman who is the true one, is lurking behind the scenes. At times you'll want him to display these Alpha Male traits, and it's unlikely that he'll be able to achieve it. You'll want him to control the situation at times , but it's not his style. Therefore, at the final analysis the Alpha Female inside you will not have the same admiration and respect that a woman ought to have for her husband. He's going to become too boring for you and you're losing attraction to him, or at the very least, be cheating on him by introducing an Alpha male. You'll be enthralled by him for being so charming and sweet however, he's not able to scratch the "itch" as you would like to, or even should it be scratched. So, guess which sleeping arrangement you'll end up at the end each day? Don't worry. There's a feasible solution to this dilemma.

We are all aware that many men, though not allwant their partner or spouse to be submissive to them. therefore, the independent Alpha Females should infuse this mantra into their love lives. "An Alpha Female on the streets and I am submissive to my husband." Hold on and hold your head up, before all of you New Age women go to roll your eyes at this book simply because I used"submissive. "submissive." The term can be beautiful when used in the right manner and in the right context with the right person. Let me hear you out for a moment before you take the "no-he-didn't" blade and slice me up to death.

Submissiveness to your partner does not mean that you are weak or inflexible, or to let him get you in trouble. Simply, it means to be submissive to your man or, as Webster Dictionary defines it, "to give up (relinquish or surrender) oneself to the authority or authority of one." By becoming submissive to your partner it means, "I recognize him as my King and leader." You're delegating the control to him. This isn't very strong by any means. It requires strength and confidence to put someone in the ability to tell them, "I will follow your instructions." In the outside of your home, your professional or workplace, be an confident Alpha Female. Be in control of your surroundings and be a self-reliant thinker. However, when you get home, or you plan for a date with your partner take off the Superwoman suit at home and simply become Lois Lane. Let us play Superman for you.

There are a few women that pop into my me when I imagine this kind of female who is submissive and Alpha. Beyonce in the beginning. She's a dominating figure in her area, however with Jay she is submissive to Jay. Mary J. Blige I consider to be this type of woman. The same goes for Michelle Obama. Women who are powerful and don't want to let their husbands lead the way. But, there's an essential element to the entire equation that must be included in order for this type of relationship to be successful and it's an essential piece of the puzzle. The person you decide to submit to be worthy of the gift. The man you choose to lead must be worthy and qualified.

I'm sure lots of women have given that wheel guy and then had him drive both of you straight into an unmarked ditch. This is the reason it is very difficult for you to give the wheel to someone else. I completely recognize this. But, here is where interaction between yourself and your prospective partner is crucial. In those dinner dates and late-night conversations it is important to let him know what you think. Tell him that you're comfortable taking on tasks by yourself however, you are not having a issue allowing your partner to take the lead. You must show you that he's not just competent in managing but also has the experience dealing with business. This is why you need to pay particular attention to the details of his daily life. There are subtle clues that can tell you the man's qualifications to steer the wheel.

First of all, do you think his hygiene and grooming practices up to scratch? If a man isn't able to take his own care and his appearance, he's probably not able to take charge of you. Does his breath smell of bad smells? Do you keep your beard and hair well-trimmed and cut? Do you have a car that is filthy and dirty both inside and out? How does his body smell? Do maintain his nails in a clean state and neat? What is his lifestyle? If he isn't able to get through this initial stage in the process of interviewing, then you may consider reconsidering your choice to be a friend. However, if you observe that he's in the right place in these aspects that he is in, then you are able to proceed to the next phase.

There's a secret my male friends are going to be furious at me for letting you know (sorry homos). Men tend to behave at their best during the first one to three months after forming a relationship, which means it's not easy to judge him on the basis of the way he behaves towards you. Therefore, you'll be forced to use other methods to assess and determine if he's capable of taking control of your car. In the beginning, observe the way he interacts with other people, specifically those that aren't really helping his cause in any way. The people you like are cashiers, waiters at the store and even strangers in the street. This allows you to check if the guy is a decent and reputable man, or is an adamant asshole. Don't give your steering wheel to an a**hole. How will he treat his grandmother and/or mother? Do they have any kind of spiritual base? This isn't talking about whether he's in the Deacon Board, or the church choir, since there are numerous dogs and devils in both posts. What I'm referring to is do you think he is a sincere prayer? Does him praise his food? The details, no matter how small they might seem, can help you get a better idea about the personality of this man. If you're satisfied with the information you have gathered during this stage then you are able to move on to the next part that will be the final interview.

Phase three is all about his spending habits, both the good as well as bad. What type of spending behavior do he have? Do you think he has an alcohol or drug addiction? What do he look like when he's drunk or high? Do you know if he has an addiction to gambling? Also, take note of his working routines. Do you find him often ending an evening conversation or phone call with you due to the fact that he needs to rise early to work the next day? Are you sure he is a dedicated worker or does he manage to do only enough to survive? Does he make his payments punctually? Do you have a complaint about his bills? or is he able to manage that business punctually every month?

These are just a few things that ladies need to take note of in deciding whether an individual is worthy of to be submissive to. What he does to your yoni while in bed shouldn't be the sole factor in determining the reason you should submit to him. Many of you commit this horrible error. Submissiveness to a man and handing over controlling authority is more an enterprise move than it is a personal one. You have handed over the business's title which includes you as well as your life's work. It is effectively hiring a CEO for your business, which is YOU. This means that there has to be a rigorous screening process that is used to determine whether the person is qualified for the job particularly if you believe that your "company" is an Fortune 500 company. Feel me?

I'm my first person to say that I believe that the normal order of things, especially when it comes to relationships between men as well as women and relationships became out of order due to our actions (or the lack of) as males. The concept of the independent woman was born and manifested when women could no longer as women, depend on us males. We couldn't rely on us to collect the money and to pay for bills. We took it out to gamble it off, played the system or smoking it up. You can't count on us to look after the child we created. You can't trust us to ensure that your livelihood and well-being was in good hands. I know that the Alpha Female was born due to the absence or absence that of an Alpha male. These identities were simply survival instincts that were kicked off due to our weaknesses.

For us to be able collectively to bring things back into their natural order, we need to pinpoint the root of the problem first, then come up with an achievable solution that can solve the problem. As we close this chapter, I would like to let all my personal Alpha Females know that I believe you are the one who can make men step back up, and in returning things to their proper view. You are the one who can convince a man to aim for the top. If you're feeling like an affluent man, but notice that he's not living up to the potential of what the man, is capable of, you can provide him with the push by telling him, "Look, I like you however, I don't believe that you're applying yourself fully currently and I'm not in a position to give you complete control as my man , and you're not making an effort to be the person I believe you could be. If you really would like to be my partner I'm going to require you prove to me that you're committed, not just to the improvement for me but also to the improvement of yourself too." Sometimes we guys need a little push from women in order to reach our full potential. Believe me, I got married to one who was able to do the same for me. While I was not in the business of handling business but I wasn't polished enough. Mentally I had one foot in the street as well as one in my business education and ideas. However, she recognized my potential and guided me to that direction without judgement or criticism.

Ladies If a man likes you and has feelings for your feelings, he'll pay attention to what you say. I guarantee you this. You'll be the fire that ignites that spark in the man that had been in a slumber, or simmering as flames of infinite potential waiting to be ignited. Some of you Alpha Females are just too strong to smother the spark of a man instead of igniting the flames. It's not my intention to ask you to take care of or soothe the mature man. Never, not ever. Certain men have to get up and shake from their mom's tit. I know this. What I'm referring to is a man with all the attributes to lead, but could be stealing those qualities, or hasn't yet been able to play the role even though it's right there in his face.

This is a gem that ladies might not be aware of about men. We all work better when given an objective. A central area. This is why you can see an innocent man transform his life around following becoming father. Now, he has a goal. He's required to look after the younger children because his mom is working. The reason is that he's been given a goal. If you've let him know what you would like from him to guide you in your direction, then you've provided him with a the opportunity to fulfill a goal that he will begin to focus on. However, here's what's important that's crucial. The person must already possess the qualities he needs. Certain men aren't made to be leaders. Somehow they aren't equipped with the skills is required to manage the household or guide women, no matter the importance you place on them. They aren't equipped to handle it. their hearts to be able to lead. You'll recognize them by the way they shy away from making any decision. You can ask him where you can go for a meal or what he would like your outfit to be, but the answer will be something like "I do not know" or "I don't really care." If you meet someone who is a bit of a hustler, who arranges your dates or gives you a list of what he wants to wear the future, you've met an individual who is able to take charge.

I am so disappointed that our generation is at an age where we need to be coaxed to be the people we are supposed to be naturally. However, because there are no fathers in the home and kids being raised by single mothers males aren't getting the mental flint required to spark that fire of determination that allows them to safeguard, care for their families as well as the women they care. However, women could be the flint. You must become the flaw. Women are reflections of their husbands But you cannot show what's not glowing.

Chapter 10: The Puppy Love

This chapter isn't about the love of a teenager which had us all caught in a dream where we believed we would have a long life and be together forever, but then the summer vacation came along and we forgot about love until the following school year began again. When I talk about "puppy loves," I want you to picture a tiny puppy who's just thrilled being loved someone as they've been sat in the pet store window for six months, alone and lonely. They don't care about their owner's name and the age they're at or what color or race they are, or the values and morals they rely on. The puppy wants to get out of that pet shop and head to a cozy home; and they'll absolutely adore you If you're the person to make it happen.

There are women that are lonely or depressed and depressed in self-esteem, that they simply need to feel loved. They'll be willing to be willing to take any man (and occasionally any woman) when they see at least a little affection. They are looking to feel loved even if they realize that it's not real love, as T.I. did so well in rapping. These women will be able to do anything, say anything, do anything, and will do anything so the person doesn't abandon them. They will be there, like a little puppy, waving their tail and jumping in your lap because you provided them with an area to call home. However, these women are destined for numerous heartbreaks and painful experience by playing the role of a housekeeper.

If a person isn't only a dog lover, or one who is kind for a puppy who is generally sweet and affectionate but over time, he will become a hater of the dog. He will begin to hate the dog. He will not accept that all that puppy desires to do is love him and eventually, he'll turn hostile towards that puppy. He'll hit it, kick it and torture it, speak of it as if it were a tyrant and everything else that is disgusting and unsavory that he could create to crush the puppy's spirit. In the end, he'll achieve exactly what he wants to do until the point that the puppy will be afraid of his presence. The puppy will be able to shed its sweet and affectionate manner of speaking. The tail will stop waving. The head will rest low instead of soaring high in the air like it did previously. It will be unable to consume anything. It will appear to be nothing more than a version of itself that was once.

If a woman is possessed of that "I just would like to feel loved" attitude and goes all in for the first person who pays her attention If he's not a person with compassion or a good character, regardless of how much the woman strives to delight his needs and to make him feel happy the man will eventually begin to dislike her like she would a puppy. He will begin to insult her, scold her, beat herup, abuse her, and disregard woman as an individual and even his wife. He will destroy all spark of light or affection that might have existed within her, causing her an empty shell of her former self.

Let's talk about the unsaid truth. Many women base their entire existence and their self-esteem on their relationships status. When they do not have a partner or aren't being attracted or courted by anyone woman, they instantly feel disqualified, unloved or unattractive. They can become desperate to find men that they begin to do things they are aware of as being completely out of their nature to try and creating a situation where a man will like or even notice them. Like a puppy that does whatever it is you ask them to do - chase balls or roll around or any other nutty technique you create in order to draw the attention of these types of women often perform all sorts of naive small "tricks" in the hope of getting that interest. Ladies I'm telling that if you are one of them most of the time you will attract the wrong type of man. This is the reason.

The majority of men who are schemers and con-artists as well as master manipulators can identify this kind of woman in a matter of miles. They are prey for these types of women. You may not realize it but one sure indicator to tell him that he's the presence of this kind of woman is when her eyes widening and she's got sparkling simply by saying"hello" or offering her an appreciation. This kind of woman is seen walking with eyes pointing toward the ground. That's the way he can tell that she's been broken. There is some women who present an appearance of confidence, obscuring their vulnerability with fake highs and a powerful attitude. Don't be fooled, ladies. don't deceive those predators. The eyes of women will reveal what's inside her each time, regardless of what she is trying to communicate with her appearance. A sad and lonely soul is unable to stop that hurt from seeingp into its owner's eyes and saturating eyes with sadness.

Ladies, the best weapon you have to protect yourself to fight loneliness and unhappy is to learn how to be in solitude. Being able to be yourself and feel a sense satisfaction and comfort. This can help you avoid many of your mistakes and reckless decisions that can cause pain and heartache. A woman who is desperate is doomed to fail. Let me repeat it. A woman who is desperate is a woman who will never be saved. It requires a particular kind of man who will attempt to first comprehend a woman who has revealed her self in this way before him and follow up with a plan to heal her, because he can recognize the beauty that lies hidden beneath her hurt. Men like this I'm not going to admit are a far cry among them. The majority of men I'm afraid to say it over and over will swindle such a woman. He will make her bleed until there is no more left in her, and then she will either go away or force her to go away. Most of the time, this kind of woman isn't willing to end their relationship regardless of how awful it's become due to the fact that she believes she's put too much in it for another woman to take him for granted.

Ladies, there's the power of knowing how to live in solitude. Being lonely and being lonely are two completely distinct things. It is important to understand this. If you're alone there are many things that have the capacity to be transparent to you as your mind and your vision are not clouded by negative or depressing feelings. You can gain a certain quality of confidence when you are at peace. You allow yourself the time to think about the exact thing you're looking for. Also, you gain some kind of respect from men who come in the contact. Few men respect a desperate woman. A woman who is too easy.

I've said before that as men we're egotistical smugglers. This is the way it is. When you surrender it in a matter of minutes in our eyes, the very first thought we have is "I am wondering if she's always this easy perhaps it's just my personal preference." In the event that we think that you're so easy for any man, it causes your to shed a amount of your sparkle with us. The majority of men need to feel that they're the only one to be special. It is believed that you act this way because you're "the men" in your perception. This is how you treat us. When you declare that you are in love with us and have not felt this way regarding anyone else this makes it more believable to us. However, if we catch suspicions that you're hungry for attention, and you'd have had the same experience with any other lullaby you've come in contact with, we'll not consider you to be "the male," just "a man," and this will make a man not get into you.

Here's an hidden truth for all the women who read this book. Everyone wants to feel that they're "the male" in the eyes of his lady regardless of age we are both. It's called the Superman Syndrome. This is the reason why the puppy love mentality is negative. You can't make everyone you meet Superman simply because he gave you some love. The people didn't label Superman for nothing simply because he was from a different planet with special abilities. Superman had actually been super. He helped people and he cared about humanity and did not use his power to do the purpose of doing harm. Do you think that they would've been calling his ass Superman even if he were killing innocent people and ruining the city? Absolutely not. The man was Superman because of his superior character and attitude. The name was earned by his appearance.

A lot of women make a man look like Superman and he's not done anything that merits this kind of treatment. He's more of an villain and you treat him as an eminent superhero. What do you think makes a good guy feel? What are the chances that you'll be in a position to make that man feel better than you did that asshole if you offered this asshole the same treatment? Let it sit for a few minutes.

I'll close with this. I personally do not think there's any issue with giving her husband unadulterated affection and love every when she meets him, as a puppy does when it meets its owner. Even if you decide to try some "tricks" to smile on the man's face, I believe this is a good way to have a stimulating as well as healthy bond. I believe that men should have earned this kind of affection and respect from his lady through his actions towards her as a woman and not just because she's looking for affection and love. If the man really is in love with his wife, he'll not ever be reluctant to earn that respect becausea genuine man will put the effort in. Feel me?

Also , ladies, stop basing your entire identity and appearance on whether or not you have a guy within your circle or otherwise. Take a look at this. The top-end cars such as Benzes, Rolls Royce, or Aston Martin don't lose their value because they're not driven. Actually the majority of wealthy people own a collection of vintage vehicles that sit at a showroom or garage, looking shiny and attractive, but seldom even driven. The cost will still be some money should you decide to purchase one of those vehicles. Therefore, the most important thing is, even if aren't married or are currently in a relationship keep it pretty and stylish, and your value won't diminish. So, neither should your self-worth or image.

For too long , we've borne the false notion that if a woman's in a relationship, there must be something not right with her. This is a false assumption that leads lots of women to make bad choices regarding men just in the interest of being in a position to claim that they are in an intimate relationship. If you let a man to shape what you are, the loss of that man's influence can make you a different person. This is also true for cars, money as well as social status and even the jobs they hold. They construct their entire identity around these things then when these things go away they sink into deep depression or, even more they try to hurt themselves.

We all desire to be loved by someone we love. We all want to feel unique to someone. I think that it's an inherent human desire. However, that need shouldn't be turned into the form of addiction (which I'll get into in a moment) that makes us go to any lengths to find the "fix." The home is the place where the heart is, therefore, ladies, if you begin to appreciate the person you are, and only you, will you never experience the feeling of being "homeless" or not loved. A woman who is in love with herself is a huge attraction for men.

Chapter 11: Love Addict

Love. A powerful elixir and soul-soother. It is as soothing as the nighttime waves that gently embrace the shore. An emotional magnet that may lure one into heaven or hell, and keep them there for the rest of their lives. Love. The most potent drug to be created. Once you've taken it, you're hooked and begging for more. It's known for making powerful men dumb and intelligent women look stupid. It's true that it's blinding, but it's is also a reminder that your heart is capable of holding the beauty of. Love. The most sought-after and sought-after thing on the planet. Every animal, rodent or mammal, wants to taste its sweet nectar. Love heals. Love destroys. Love deceives. Love can blind, but it can also unite two souls as a woven quilt. It is felt across the longest distances and across the most dense walls. It's been the cause of many warsbut has have ended only a handful. What exactly is love? It's a beautiful and tragic event that everybody seems to be into love.

One thing I've observed is the lack of affection from a man can leave women cold, hateful and hard and distant. A lot of women's attitude is based only on whether they're being appreciated. Be attentive to women when they enter involved in a new relationship. She's happy, glowing smiling, and an ray of sunshine. She's not bothered by anything or cause her to get angry. She's the most charming woman you'll meet. But, do you run into that same woman six or eight months later as the relationship is beginning to fall apart. She'll probably not be so lovely when she's there. She'll be irritable, rude curt, and isn't interested in being at all.

Many women don't realize the fact that allowing your relationship status to influence your manner of speaking and your emotions can impact more than your mood. It can impact your relationship with coworkers as well as your work attitude It can also impact the way you spend your money (some women spend more when they're unhappy) and could impact the relationship you have to your kids. There women who take the blame on their children whenever their husbands start acting out. This anger and frustration carries onto the one the closest your heart, i.e. your children in the event that you have any.

Lack of love can cause a woman to become savage. It can lead her to turn into a unhappy person if she is not in tune with her. It can cause her to be trapped in a completely unnatural situation. Some women will even go on the prowl or completely avoid men. Sharp edges begin to develop around their once jolly persona. The light that used to make her to shine like a ray of sunshine slowly begins to fade. Their smile fades. They're no longer accessible to male who may have an some interest in their lives. Her heart has become hard and is now closed to any avenues leading to it.

When I consider women who exhibit the same kind of behavior as well as conduct immediately brings me back to an alcohol or drug addict. When addicts are able to access their drink or drug of choice, they're the most happy and content people in the world (except for those who are violent when drunk or high). For them, life is good and all is well. Their troubles have gone away and disappeared. However, should the addict be unable to obtain the substance or drink they desire and what happens? They get depressed, angry and very angry. Some are even violent. The entire state of their mind is determined by that substance or drink.

In this way many women do not even realize they've become addicted to love. They've developed a dependency on the sensation of being in love or the feeling of love for someone. They're the same dependent upon being in relationships, as an addict of the substance. Just like the addict to drugs whose addiction has grown so strong that they'll take a hit of everything in the name of being the high. A woman's desire to love for someone else can be so strong that she'll be willing to give all her heart to anyone simply for the sake of love for someone. If she's not in love with one person, she can begin to feel inadequate, useless insignificant, unworthy, and inadequate. Everything about her as well as her well-being is directly dependent on the person she's in love with. She is driven to feel valued and loved by men.

I'd like to share a line with you , which is from the bestseller Anam Cara (did you Goggle it?) composed by John O'Donohue. The text states "You will never be able to love someone else until you're equally involved in the wonderful, but challenging, spiritual process of finding yourself to love . . . You don't have to leave your home to find out what love is."

This is a important and powerful message to live by. When you learn to first love yourself you are able to make your own decisions with regard to your love life. Your moods and emotions are no longer influenced by the quality of your relationship since you've discovered the abundance of love in yourself. When you learn to be yourself, if you meet someone worthy of your affection the affection you show him will be a reflection of the love that you've embedded in your own.

Additionally, once you've learned to be a lover of yourself, you'll never accept certain behaviours and actions from men. Women often do this because they're so dependent on their man being present in their lives to ensure that they have someone they can love and they don't wish to go away from this. Therefore they are more likely to accept all the crap that this man feeds them on a regular basis, much like an addict copes with the unpleasant sensation that their descent will give them. To them, it's an amount to pay for the feeling of euphoria the high brings to them. In reality, the man's trash is a minor cost to pay, as at least you're the man in your life who is trustworthy, right?

Being a true lover of yourself also creates the confidence because, when you realize the self-love that is within you, it will begin to shatter the fears that weighed on your mind and soul. You've come to appreciate your beauty which is directly affecting the self-esteem and self-esteem of yours. If a man decides to cut off his connection with your life the account won't be empty, which will cause you to feel empty and feeling of loneliness. You'll have an "back-up reservoir" that is in your soul which you can draw from for the sake of keeping your bank account and your heart. You're no longer dependent on a man's affections. It eliminates the feelings of despair, neediness and the need to be loved. It is now something that is a strength rather than being a weakness, it is a benefit instead of being a burden. It's now an asset rather than an obstacle.

Also, you will no longer suffer from those erratic mood swings that typically are directly linked to the way your partner is treating you. You're being bullied by your man out and you decide to go around and blast on your children. Your husband didn't show up last night, and you lash out at your coworker at work. The man splurged on the cash to pay the bill, and now you're blaming the cashier who is ringing you up with a slow ring. If your man isn't reciprocating the gratitude you've shown to him, and which you're dependent upon, his actions (or the lack of it) could turn you into an unwelcome little troll and no one would like being in your presence. Even your children.

Don't let a person remove that sweetness from your heart. Don't let his incompetence hinder your caring and compassionate spirit. Being yourself is the only way to be free. If he notices that you aren't willing to accept certain things, he'll not be able to attack you in any type of manner. When he realises, it's true that you be in love with him however, you don't really need it for survival He'll be more aware of his behavior since he is aware that you're not having any concerns about leaving him.

Let me spill the unspoken truth to you here. I'm asking you to be attentive to this point. Man can tell the presence of an unbreakable relationship with a woman who will not let him go regardless of what she does. We can recognize you love addicts fast and profit from your addiction.

All of us require love and to be loved. Our souls long to be loved. Love enhances us. It helps us live. It lets us open the lid on the sarcophagus that been encased in darkness. It transforms our lives and forces us to confront the world's challenges with a gleeful grace. It's pretty on us. It is a pleasant feeling to us. However, it's one of the most important sources of all our pain and heartache stems from. The addiction is slowly destroying us physically and mentally. When you develop a an affection for yourself It does not just improve your life, it also helps you stay in a healthy state. It helps you maintain a solid base to stand on when you're being on the edge of love's ledge and helps you avoid getting swept off.

As a society, we must be aware that sexual sex and a desire to be loved could be a dangerous mix as is mixing sleeping pills and alcohol. If you don't and you don't realize it it's likely that you'll find yourself "strung up" and pretending to be waiting for the subsequent "hit." The next moment, you'll be giving your man more than you'd ever thought to give. You're taking on more than you thought you could be able to. You're far too much, yet it makes your body feel amazing. It's a miracle that he hits you exactly the way you prefer it to hits. The way he makes it happen on you, he's got to want to get to know you, right? As time passes, you begin to fall in love, not him but the sex game and how you feel when he is around. After a hard day's work, you're in need of that you need that, don't you?

When you've had to deal with the naughty sexually abused kids, you're craving the freedom you're sure he'll grant you True? You're not just addicted to it however, you're also dependent upon it. It's possible that he's an asshole or a bad dog at any time however, when you're asleep, he can make your body twitch and then burst with ecstasy, particularly when he's ecstasy-bound. In the 30 to 60 minutes, he's your man. Believe me, I've been there so I know.

You are captivated by the way the guy can make you feel sexually as a drug addict would love any drug can make them feel happy and lets them escape the troubles and worries of life for a few minutes. You don't have to be embarrassed about this. Everyone has their own demons and flaws. However, it's high time you stop faking it and recognize that it's what it is. It's the only way to be able to break the addiction. There are some who may require to enter into sexual rehabilitation also known as celibacy to get your head straight and get a better understanding of the reasons why you are constantly in certain situations with males.

This will also allow you time to understand about, understand, and love yourself. There are some of you who should consider being honest with yourself and acknowledge that good lingam can make you weak. The thought of a good chunk of flesh, no matter in the case of an unsatisfactory man, triggers you to leave your sphere, and perhaps could cause that you see more of that person than what's actually there. It's time to be honest with you about what factors have an effect on you in your relationships, and the reasons why they have an impact on you. The expression "know your self" is among the most wise quotes ever written and it can be extremely beneficial to your daily life. Learn to love yourself and know your self. This will give you the strength to stand up to the test and challenges. If you want to be loved by someone or be accepted by them, head out and purchase the puppy. They're not as expensive and require are a lot less trouble.

Also, I'd like you to think about becoming an addict to love from this perspective. It makes you an enabler. Have you ever met parents or parents who would like their child to be liked by their child enough that they let the child to do what they'd like to do and say whatever they'd like to and act however they like and acquire whatever they wish to acquire? This child probably develops into an unkind, rude and disrespectful brat. The parents of the child did not hold the child accountable for his actions and he didn't have to fight for the privileges that he got in life.

When you ladies allow the man-child to do whatever is his will, do whatever he's looking for, or say whatever he's thinking about all because you're addicted by your sexual activity, or simply being a woman on your bed in the night, you're subconsciously creating the same obnoxious rude, uncaring, reckless brat who's never capable of becoming an adult with a sense of responsibility because you did not hold the man to account for what he did. Did you remember the film Baby Boy? This is the reason we see so many grown males who are at home with Call of Duty on the Xbox throughout the day, while women are working. She's happy with him being at home in the event that he keeps an eye on her kids while working. She will buy videos, marijuana, and anything else he's in need to be able to bring him home after she comes back. If he is able to watch the kids and let her experience an every two days orgasmic and she's satisfied, she's satisfied. Does this really what relationships have become? Do you think this is the current image of manhood? Are the roles reversed? It certainly appears so.

Ladies, they might be more difficult to come across as unicorns and leprechauns however, there are men available to you that you could become addicted to. One who will for that cash, assist with the expenses, help with your kids, and yet make you want to have two or three times a every day. All without complaining or a grumble. Don't let your desire to be loved cause you to give up on less. Don't be afraid to accept that consolation prize. Remember that the "Grand Prize" is still available It's not just that it available and you're entitled to be able to claim it!

Chapter 12: The Assault On The Temptress

Before I start this chapter, I'd like to define the meaning of the term "Temptress. It's the woman who is entices or in other words that entices men to commit a sin or act recklessly. The woman that entices or appeals to men even when she knows he's married or has a relationship with one of his partners already. Okay, let me apologize for my behavior because I'm about to step onto toes that have been trimmed by the end of this chapter.

We've come across the woman we are talking about by numerous names, including hoe man-stealer and the mistress to mention some. However, regardless of the title the actions and behavior are quite similar to each other. It is this woman that plans and enjoys being a sexy or sexually attractive partner to someone who is not her own. She's not shy about dissolving a marriage or creating a gap the relationship of a couple. The only thing she cares about is her own desires and wants. Some women are unforgiving. They really don't want to be with the person they're dating or sleeping with, they simply want to wipe the smile the woman might smile at because she believes or believed it was a happy relationship. The woman who is in the process wants to feel the joy of being in a position to say, "Yeah, she thought that her boyfriend was all that and I'm certain that he's nothing more than an animal."

This is a woman who is adamant about crushing dreams and destroying dreams. This is the homegirl who claims she only chats with married men because she is able to "play together for a few hours before sending his sex on to the wife of his." In plain English she does not have to confront his sexuality outside of possibly earning a bit of money from him. The sexy woman is the one who is willing to sleep with her cousin's boyfriend behind her back or her husband from her best friend in a low-key manner or even her mother's boyfriend, if he's attractive enough. There is no man not acceptable to her.

Let's dig deeper You are not here to judge or even to make judgments. My job is to define what is and how it could be a hindrance with regards to finding real love. I'm sure being the lover can be extremely satisfying and satisfying for some who claim to be in this position. If this is the way you decide for your own life and you're seeking nothing more important for yourself, then this book isn't the one for you, but I appreciate you making the effort to check it out. If, however, you find yourself in this position and secretly long for something with more substance We'll try to delve into all those feelings of disappointment and pain so we can discover the reason that inspires you to become "The temptress."

Be aware of this, but I do believe that there's an important distinction from a girl who takes the wrong choice of sleeping with a different man because of loneliness, or a girl who lures men, even though they know that they already is a part of another woman. However, be aware that with the right ingredients the latter can be, and frequently is made into a sexual attraction. Women are emotional beings and, at times, they are lost in the web of emotions and want attention and love where it isn't needed as your friend's boyfriend. The emotions of women are amplified and increased when a woman is in a state of loneliness, despair or both. It's the time when most women commit mistakes when it comes to concerns of the heart when they're feeling lonely or depressed. This is when any kind of attention is acceptable. However, this kind of woman usually isn't initially a fling but she is a woman with the potential of being one. I'll tell you why this is.

Sure, some lovers are created by an amalgamation of loneliness and their closest friend, sister or cousins telling them all about their work. That's right I did it. There are many women who make your lonely or depressed closest friend or sister or cousin into a flirt (although not knowing it) by revealing every detail of the interactions with your partner at night. Be aware that when you're describing the details in detail to your favorite friend either your sister, cousin, or best friend the extent to which the man's "ego" is as well as how he operates to build that ego, how great his tongue is, or how impressive his endurance is, your the best friend, sister or even your cousin might not be seeing any performance like that. In fact, they you may not even know what to do to get any action similar to this. In fact it's the case that she's not seen anything similar to that in a time, so while you're putting the tape back to your amazing "sexcapades," she's secretly thinking that she could be in the shoes of you. You'll never be able to tell this because she's confident that you that you can count on her, isn't it?

Ladies, listen up. If you are willing to divulge every detail of your man's sexual preferences to your unhappy, desperate and gorgeous best friend or sister and the more likely she's likely to begin fantasizing about your guy in those dark, evenings. Now, when she meets him, she's viewing him in a different perspective. She's now aware of the contents of the comfortable jeans he's wearing and the way he wears with it. When he casually is licking his lips around her then she thinks about how great that tongue could feel against her. She doesn't see him as the one who is that she is currently dating or who has married her best friend, sister or even a cousin. He is now looking and appears much more appealing.

I've had several instances where I could tell precisely when a girl I was with had revealed to the best of her friends or sister or even a cousin about me and my sexual habits, since initially they would say "Hey D. What's up boy?" then they became, "Mmph. Everyone's not able" and were looking me around. I could sense the eyes turning on their heads whenever I'd see them look at me from the corner of their eyes. I also could sense that she had more knowledge regarding me than she could have. Before I get started I'll give a short story to you in order to illustrate how this situation has occurred before.

In the year 1997, I was in a room at the home of one my friends, and his girlfriend (who is supposed to have been expecting by him). I was aware that she was a fan of my son, and we formed the brother/sister kind of relationship as a result of it. Then, one day, my friend was detained in a minor scuffle involved several other guys in the complex. Of course I took over to supervise her and the place until he was released. One day she asked me whether I would like to go to the house of her cousin. She told me that I was holed in my house to supervise her the majority of the time, so she believed that I would benefit from some "female company." I was happy with that, so we went to pick the cousin up.

But, remember it was 2 weeks now since my dear was locked up So I'm sure the it was clear that loneliness (and excitement) was beginning to creep into my the sis. Of course, my cousin and I did our thing in the evening and that was it. So, I thought. I'm assuming that my cousin returned and revealed the majority of my "sexual information" to my girlfriend from my house since, while I was smoking outside and smoking a cigarette the girl from my house took me to her apartment. When I entered I noticed that she and her cousin were sitting on the couch together and I was instructed to sit in the seat directly across from them. Unsure of what was happening I settled down. My friend's daughter was looking at her cousin and asked, "You want to tell him what you think, or do I let him know?" By this time I'm wondering what is happening. So, my homie's girlfriend finally tells me, "Don't worry, I'll let him know." She looks at me straight in the eyes and then says, "If it was up for me, I'd have had you fucked up." She stunned me with her brilliance and brilliance, and stunned me by her words. It was a girl I observed how ferocious she was for my homi. However, I think loneliness combined with her sister talking to her about me and my company made her a sexy person and the hottest girl in her life. She never came near to talking or even look at me in that manner. I told her that she was tripping and then walked out.

The main point of this story is to be mindful of the amount of bedroom information you share with your closest family members, friends and cousins. It's possible that no one else will have the wild, thrilling and soul-stirring sex as you're having. All you're doing is promoting the sexuality of your man. You're inadvertently entice your most cherished friend or sister and could cause her to transform into a sexy fling.

Let's go to the opposite kind of a woman. The kind who doesn't require any of your guy's sexual characteristics to tempt her to lure him. It's because she's in love with him. Another woman goes interested in seeing if can get a man to bed her. It's a prank for her. This woman is more risky in comparison to the person I mentioned. She's more than predator. She observes your husband is weak, and then is looking for weaknesses in his character, then uses it to her advantage. Her aim is to get your husband's or man's eyes wide open for her. They are like prized possessions for her. Conquests. What is it that makes women want to intentionally destroy or interfere with the relationship or marriage of another woman? I have told you in several chapters in the past that when you encounter women with these characteristics or similar, they were either taught to look like this conscious or unconsciously or created through a number of hurts and heartbreaks. It was a lot of pain, suffering, and sorrow to look like this.

Her mother might have taught her when she was a young girl not to believe in men. It could have been taught to ever give her heart to any man in the world. Use him for what he's worth , and allow him to go regarding his own business. It could be that she's resembling what she observed in her younger years and thought that was the best way to go. There was some big sisters or an aunt was someone she admired who also acted in the same manner and she followed the footsteps of her predecessors. You could have offered your heart and soul to women time and over only to see it be smashed, cut in half, or torn from her chest which is why she's chosen to handle a different man since there isn't time to be worrying her over anything, and this is the truth that is not spoken about. The majority woman is afraid of becoming emotionally attached to men, and that is the reason why she prefers to choose to go with a different man, since, in her opinion it is unlikely that he'll be emotionally attached to her as there is already an individual at home. However like I've said earlier certain women are sad and broken that they do not desire the idea of seeing another female be happy. This in itself isn't a safe area to be in. The kind of hatred and snarkiness can cause an illness in the body of a woman and cause a swell of discomfort throughout her soul.

Be aware and remember that if you find yourself in this category or are identified with this kind of woman I'm not here to make judgments about you. There is likely to be something in you and your heart that requires to be healed or forgiven and that's the thing I want you to uncover. I'll tell you me: "I don't really care about what you have--a car, house, a pair shoes, or even a man, there's something as good as having your own. and a queen must be able to have her very own.

Here's a double dose of the unspoken facts for ladies to drink. There are a lot of Queens out there are choosing the job of concubine. Let me go back. Many of you gorgeous Queens in the world are now settling to play the role of a concubine. Oh, I can be hearing the choruses "No I did not" and "No he didn't. It's true, I did it, Ms. Lady. that is the reason I did.

A concubine can be defined as "a woman who lives with the man with who the woman isn't married. the second wife." In essence, the women who are flirts and side-kicks are like concubines in the modern world. The King calls you when he's exhausted of making his wife suffer and, after getting his feet clean and sends you back to your home, and then returns home to his Queen. So, I'm asking you, what is the reason that so many of you queens choosing to play the part of the wife? Do you think your fear of rejection and pain really resulted in you falling so far from your marital goals? Big Brotha Jah believes that it's past the time to get yourself up, put your head, put on a crown and get yourself the King you want to call your own instead of just an ounce of it. That's what a queen is truly entitled to. Before I end this chapter I'd like you to think about this question, and think for a moment on your answer. What kind of elegant, classy woman with respect for herself would ever settle for receiving a small portion of a man's body? Better yet, how about in sloppy minutes?

Many of you who are career-driven and goal-oriented women out there think that you don't have the time to tolerate these idiots who aren't trying to be a failure in their lives and believe they're only good at just one thing. You ain't got time right? It's simpler to close your eyes and get it to go away. I can sense that. You might feel that the woman who is cheating on him is her fault rather than yours. What I find most confusing about women who have a relationship with a woman's boyfriend is what has happened to the code of conduct and the unity of the sisterhood?

I see women unite over social issues, such as women's rights, such as the Women's March and the #MeToo movement, but you'll take each other's throats and slits in front of a man, often, a man who's not even yours. You fight against injustices and wrongdoings committed against you by those in power or corporate institutions however when you are capable of achieving an orgasm or even a touch of affection it's not a thought about the harm it's going cause the wife of that man when she learns of your actions. You don't think about the consequences for her family's livelihood or even her own. If you force him to be divorced or persuade him to obtain one, what happens to her children and her?

What is it that women can do to fight in such a way and with pride against the forces that oppose their rights, and then turn to be the cause of another woman's suffering? It's like me being proudly marching at an Black Lives Matter rally, then taking the opportunity to shoot the club during the weekend. You shouldn't be marching and screaming for women's rights only to claim that right from them. No matter if you believe it or not, the woman whose husband or man you're staking out and perhaps even praying for, deserves to be content. Even if the husband is weak and just looking for a bit of fun She has the right to be able for a successful marriage, without being able to make it any more difficult to save it by encouraging his reckless behaviour by offering the man an invitation to the forbidden fruit. Let me ask you this. If every man who tried to cheat his spouse or girlfriend was rejected by each woman he approached, with whom would he be cheating with his wife? If women weren't playing the role of a temptress Bonnie to every cheating Clyde What would the difference in relationships be? Of course, I'm sure that this won't be the case, but in the event that one woman did have an alteration of mind about pursuing, stalking or even seducing a woman's husband following the reading of this chapter, I believe that the ink was not wasted.

There are always temptations in our daily lives, as every temptation originates in us. Therefore, I am aware that a woman who is a temptress cannot lure men who don't desire to be enticed. I am aware that the germinated in the man before she even came across his path. It was only her job to bring to the surface what was already manifesting in his soul through himself and his thoughts. Trust me, I've played what I am doing inside out. I could have smacked an entire nation with my actions but I chose to work for to liberate our people. Therefore, I'm not placing blame entirely on you. I would like to encourage you to live a happier and satisfying life. Not being the source of unhappy or unhappy person is a way to live a happier life. We aren't able to influence anyone else's behavior however we can take control of our personal. The point is that, just when you spot dogs preparing to escape from the house and you're not required become the person to take him away and let him out of the gate.

Chapter 13: "Catch And Release"

If you aren't familiar with the concept of "catch and release" let me introduce you to the concept. "Catch and Release" is the phrase employed in the field of fishing. There are private fishing farms that permit you to fish in their waters however, they might have the catch and release rule which means that you are able to catch any fish you like however you aren't able to keep the fish. You have to release them back into the waters for others to take. This is generally for people who simply enjoy the game of fishing and don't care about the catch to eat.

There are ladies, whether you know you or not who are prone to a catch and release attitude when it comes down to dating men and. You'll meet a man who you like and you'll take all the steps to "catch" his attention or attention, but if you are able to capture him in whatever way you had in mind gradually, you begin to lose the attraction to him. In no time, you'll be releasing him to the dating pool only to be pursued by a new woman.

Women who have this kind of mindset usually are more interested in "the pursuit" of the male and not the man. They want to know whether they can get the man of a certain type to be drawn towards them as well as they believe that the "bigger they can catch," is better. This is purely an ego-boosting act for her. Yes, women play this game. The men aren't the only players when it comes to games such as these. Women love having their self-esteems to be boosted and brushed. Therefore, catching a male particularly if he appears to be impossible to catch and prone to being a huge self-esteem and ego booster for women of the same age. But there's a tidbit of fact. The more difficult he tries to be caught, the more her fascination with the man's abyss.

Ladies I'm going to expose to you a little in this post, as it's time to get our closets cleaned. Our marriages and relationships are messy because many of our peculiar closets are filthy. If a man is in a relationship with women with this specific idiosyncrasy is to be able to get by and the faster she's likely to be able to stop her interest. Fishing for sport is a sport for fishermen. are known to put in the effort to play their sport. This is where the excitement of the game is fighting and wrestling to land the fish in his net or boat. This makes the winning and the triumph over the entire experience more satisfying and enjoyable. If a fish shows up and jumps into the boat, it's likely to release it back into the water. The thrill is in the thrill of catching something that doesn't wish to be caught or isn't caught. When someone has set their goals upon the "fish," and she has thrown her line in the water the more difficult he will be to catch and catch, the more she'll struggle and fight to capture him. She hopes to achieve that egotistical win of catching someone who was highly sought-after or was almost impossible to capture. Also "wild games."

This could be a part of the psychological reason that explains why women are drawn to thugs, bad guys, or even men who may be wild around their edges. They're wild game to them. They don't want to be captured. A few men I've spoken with are unable to grasp why women be with a guy for the rest of her life who is constantly hounding her or making her miserable and then decide to walk away with a nice guy without hesitation. This is the reason. Women who have the catch and release mindset become involved in their own games, particularly when they're the "big award." She desires not really needs the satisfaction of putting him on the hook. The satisfaction of getting there and "getting the man of her dreams." Sometimes it can take her two three or five years to catch him, but once caught up in the pursuit and is determined to win, it's difficult to let go of the chase, as she isn't willing to let him go. However, once the man finally does accept her offer and let her get him in the end, the game is over and the thrill of the chase fades away and the desire in him to fade slightly.

Before I got married I would always hear people telling me not to marry. As soon as I got married, things would change. I was unable to comprehend this, because I thought the same way. If two people love each in a way where they want to marry and live the entire life together How could the love and attraction suddenly disappear? This never made sense for me until I started to think about it from a perspective of catch and release.

In our culture women are criticised and judged based on the reality of whether they are able to find married or not. There is a reason why women are viewed as or thought to be broken or damaged or even tainted in the event that they don't find married. This is why a lot of women, often subconsciously, switch on the"catch-and-release" button in their heads in order to ensure they don't get seen by society in a negative manner. They put their names out into the dating pool with great force and sometimes with a ferocious determination in the hope of securing the attention of a potential partner (husband). Their main objective is to bring an individual to marry which makes the man look to be more of an accessory rather than an actual husband. She'll do all the things that need to be done in order to get her husband. Naturally, once the man lets himself be caught, believing he's the perfect opportunity and she is able to get her wedding date and her husband and the ink has dry on the marriage certificate and her goal is completed, she's accomplished which is why she quickly sheds the cloak and shows him her real self. Ladies, I can see you shouting, "Men do it too," and you are completely right. However, this will be discussed with me and the guys in a future book. I'm focusing on you at the moment.

Let me assure you ladies, and you could go to the bank. You who exhibit this kind of mindset and exhibit this kind of behavior, are ruining men for ever. You're creating bitter men who are feeling cheated and also feel like a shrewd fool. I'm sure you're constantly speaking about Girl Power and sticking together however you are essentially creating a selection pool that is which is as small as it is for other females. Particularly if the man hasn't ever been loyal to his family, but eventually decides to get together for the woman believes to be worthy however, once you get your feet on the ground and attempt to be a good guy and is a fool, she is a complete fool him. I've seen this happen many times over. It's true that I am able to hear the majority you screaming, "His dog ass deserved it. It's Karma returning to his back," but where does this kind of thinking bring us in the overall world of affairs? The game we're playing must be ended at some point and someone must start the process. I am appealing to you ladies in the first place since I know you are more educated, mature, and well-informed among us. It's not possible to keep playing to tat, you injured me and I hurt you. This is because we aren't the ones who are losing. It's our kids who will suffer the most from the stupid games we engage in. I'm going to digress I suppose, but it was simply being in my head. Now, let's get let me return to the topic to be given.

Let me offer you ladies an insider hint. Men do not like being ridiculed. Some have even been killed for it. This is the primary reason behind why certain men from committing their hearts to women. If the man does finally take that huge leap and decides to offer all of himself towards a female, it isn't an easy thing for the emotional side of him, but typically, he does it due to the fact that a woman has demonstrated her some sort of character that have provided him with the confidence to make the decision. However, if you women turn around and toss him back into the dating pool because you have lost the attraction for him, because you believe you've were able to get what you wanted then you're throwing an piranha, a shark and a barracuda into the pool that is going to devour any woman who happens to be able to catch him.

Women need to learn to eliminate the idiosyncrasies that prevent people from finding (and maintaining) the love of your life and a lasting relationship. We need to change this irrational thought process that seems to cover our minds. The man has no motivation to be a good person in the event that he knows that in the event that he drags you along and does not allow you to completely catch him and you'll always be ahead of him. Our priorities are off-base, chasing people who do not want us, and ignoring those who are. I've mentioned this before in the book however I'd like to be sure to reiterate this here. God will not give you a gentleman when you continue to throw away and getting rid of the ones that you do get. It's high time you quit dating for fun and instead, start dating for an objective.

A majority of us desire love however, in reality we're scared of it, that's what causes all these emotional idiosyncrasies and symbiosis to out of us. We're hurting each other and ourselvesmentally, emotionally spiritually and emotionally, and until we start to tackle this issue with honest and sincere commentary and discussions the damage is going to get worse and more severe. Every raindrop doesn't feel it's responsible for the flooding. I've said that neither we women or men want to believe that we are responsible in the floods of sorrow and heartache that flows like a raging stream through our souls. The relation between women and men has turned into a massive heap of emotional shit which is why the only method improve is someone making their hands dirty and then sifting it out.

That being said, ladies, if you feel that you aren't ready for an actual relationship, let the man know. If you're sure that you're not attracted to a guy and aren't ready to go on a ride with him for the whole time and leave him on the table to allow another woman who is prepared for the challenges that come from being in love. Women of a mature age take and hold. Children who are scared of the water take a catch, and let it go. However, it's fine when you're fearful or nervous. A new relationship could be scary. The process of starting over can cause people to feel a bit scared. That's understandable. Therefore, why don't you be keeping that "fishing net" away from the water until you conquer or resolve the problems make you fearful? At the very least, tell the man you love, "Hey, I'm not trying to take you away. I'm just starting to get started in the world of dating So I'm just trying to get to know my way around."

Before I close this chapter, I'd like to offer a brief jewel for those women who are supposed to release and catch however, don't. There are occasions when that you must catch and release. There are those who pull the "alligator gars" "water moccasins" as well as "snapping turtles" from the dating pool and carry the fish home with you like you've caught a an all-star catch. They bite you up to five time before you realise that you have to let them go at the side of the road. (Don't return them to the pool. Now, stop it!). Many women require to become more "fishermen." Get off the hook! Stop drag home shit out of the pool that no woman wants to consume (date). They are bottom feeders, scavengers and parasites. Let's conclude this chapter with an unspoken fact that is incorporated to the current climate This is true only applicable to. If women came with a more effective bait, you could get a bigger fish. Hello! !

Chapter 14: No Cost Jewels

As I bring the book to an end I'd like to make use of this final chapter to chat with readers about some of the thoughts that might give you a new perception and outlook on certain things that happen in your life. Let me first affirm that I'm not above these men I talk about within this article. While I've never hurt women physically, I am aware that I could have left damage or scars that can sometimes be the most devastating wounds that leave. This is what made the book since I have a gorgeous step-daughter that is set to enter the world as a young woman, and I'd prefer a man not to treat her the way I've done to women. But, I do not want her to make the same mistakes I've witnessed so many women do during my life due to being alone or desire to be loved.

The book was also written by me to help us raise one another up both as women and men. We need to realize how our choices as human beings can affect each other. I will never be able to excuse myself for my choices as a young man however, I am able to say that my perspective on relationships was influenced by women. I was surrounded by women including my aunts and cousins and the local church that I was raised in, and the homegirls I was raised with. I was always fascinated and intrigued by females. However, it also allowed me to discover the "not very attractive" aspect of women too. This is the side that women are afraid to show their male. Don't be a fool and pretend you don't understand what's going on. Being a young man led me to develop confidence issues with women which, in turn, shaped my attitude and beliefs about relationships. My ethos was "I'ma take her before she's got me."

I've seen my cousin's baby mama trying to hand me the yoni in front of him. I've witnessed my best friends' girlfriends and cousins toss it at me in a sly manner. I've had women reveal to me their thongs when their husband was not looking. It's also happened to me that I was one of the "other guy." Therefore, as there are so many women accusing us of being a sexist jerk Perhaps it's time to sweep your front porch.

Let me share to you ladies that I have had the pleasure of reading. It is in the novel The Game of Life and How to Play It by Florence Scovel Shinn. She wrote: "Many people, however they are unaware of their own destiny and are chasing certain things and events that are not theirs which will result in disappointment and failure if they achieve."

This is a inspiring quote for me with regard to women and the relationships they have. A lot of women are seeking, and settling for men who aren't theirs And I don't mean by the meaning of "he's got married." In terms of the person you are and you want to be, some men do not fit with either, or are part of your future. They're not meant to suit you. As humans we have a desire for the things (and whom) we like. We're stubborn, just like the rest of us. This is the main reason why many relationships fail and cause frustration. It is important to be aware of your identity and what you're trying to achieve in your life. What can you tell which man is suitable for you if you don't know who you are? Like, when you get to know your body, and listen to your body, it'll inform you when it doesn't agree with what you've eaten when you begin to know your self and the spirit in your being, that spirit will inform you when it's not in harmony with the person you've selected.

Take note of this. I'm sure I'll be ridiculed by men who say the above, yet I am convinced that women make men better. A strong, uncompromising woman can entice or even men be more proactive and perhaps even increase his level of maturity. In the Bible and other gnostic writings wisdom is always described as the woman. They proclaim wisdom by using "her" or "she." The latter I believe is not by chance. Women are the embodiment of wisdom, in my opinion. In theory, I believe that's the reason why women mature quicker than men. You're all wise however, you're also emotionally and that's where conflict can arise. You'll give up your knowledge to pursue the love of your life. You'll abandon your wisdom in pursuit of an enjoyable orgasm. Being lonely is the most destructive thing you can do to your knowledge. This is the cause of all discord between males and females in relationships.

I am also convinced that women are assigned to teach us men about love. Before you begin to trip I'll just be there for a moment. Who first is teaching a boy about love? Mother or father? Who teaches him to be kind and sweet? Who is the one who teaches him good manners as well as how to behave girls? His mother. She is the foundation and the woman who is his one to help him build the house that love has built. However, I want to stress this: that a man needs to have certain traits in his personality and spirit in order for the relationship to function harmoniously.

Take note of this. Men will not keep doing what is known to be unacceptable to his wife. accept, if he truly cares about her. If he doesn't really give an inch about her, then he'll simply leave her. However, a man who is devoted and loves his wife, will be a good listener to her . . . The majority of the time (Hey there's still a lot of boneheads from time to time). Therefore, if the woman is able to keep her well-maintained, emotionally and spiritually stable and has a gorgeous spirit her words will be able to have a lot of weight for her partner. She can then show him how she deserves to be loved and inform him that if he's incapable of doing this and she is not able to do that, she will leave. The problem is that sitting in silence and accepting the nonsense of a man is not just a way to destroy this woman as well, it could slow the growth of that man because he'll believe that it's okay to behave in this manner because she's accepting the fact that it is acceptable.

It's exactly the same as the case where a man suckers in bed, however women accept the fact that she is sucking and doesn't say any thing about it. She just pretends to be a victim. What can he do to know it's actually him who does suck? Then, he lays another woman, and does the same and she does not speak out to avoid bruising his ego. She then attempts to fake it as well. Soon, the man will be convinced that they're a lot of fun in bed, even though it's true that he is a suck! Many men, for this reason, believe that they're doing a good job with their partners, yet they're actually getting sucked into. Why? Because a woman hasn't admitted to him that he's a suck. Women will accept a lot from men because they want to have men.

Like how ladies are taking on a much more open approach to their bedroom by giving a man the information you'd like and the things that make you feel good and happy, you must also adopt a more vocal approach to what you would like in your relationship. What you'll and won't not be able to accept. Be unmoved by the rules. Communication is the most important element of relationships. It is often lacking. Nobody is truly honest about their motives. There's a lot of smoke and mirrors, but to what purpose? To be capable of playing house with your spouse? A lot of marriages are based on an "friends benefiting from" concept.

Ladies, we're the ones who lead everything else, but you should be the ones to lead in the issue about the soul. Men are generally poor in relationships. It's not something we are good at. Women are needed to lead us through this area of our lives. But, you need to remain pure in your behavior as well as your actions. Being a part of this "If you're not able to beam them to join 'em, then join 'em" attitude is not going to get anyone but us anywhere. All we'll accomplish is to destroy the home and family structure. We need to return to those traditional values that our grandfathers and grandmothers were able to have. They didn't get together for fifty, forty and sixty years without a reason. They worked hard and worked as a group to achieve that one common goal of maintaining and raising the family together.

It is still possible to love. In spite of the sexually-driven society that we live in. However, love begins in the soul. True love begins with self. It starts in the confines of your self-image, and later expands to an individual. You can show your love in the way that you would like to receive. Find a person who has a personality that is similar to your personal style. The key is compatibility in the world of romance. Do not try to squeeze your square peg into the hole in the shape of the shape of a circle. Maintain an open-mind and an openhearted heart. You never know what kind of color or height or weight your soulmate could be.

You don't have a choice and you could find the right partner.

True love does not have limits, or even obstacles. It's fluid and mutable and it's extremely difficult to locate. It is difficult to find the true love of your life; it appears at the time you most likely won't, and in the most unlikely of places. This is why it's so gorgeous.

For the men who may be in the process of reading this book, be sure to meditate in this. It's time to stop playing. It's time to get our females and mold them into the Queens they're meant to be. If we don't the process continues to be the way Tupac had predicted it--"We'll be a nation of children who will be averse to women who create their children." Kings create. Boys destroy. We'll rap more often in very near time. The Man's Character is coming soon to your mind.

I'm a proponent for creating stronger bonds between women and men because I believe that it's all mutually beneficial. It is possible to gauge the strength of a country by how its children and women are treated.

Strengthen the woman and she will help the children. That will certainly create a secure future for the kids since they represent the future. If our homes remain broken, the nation will be in the end broken. Children will suffer since, when a woman who's mother suffers the heartbreaks, and the men's rejections It's not just her who is suffering as much as her children. It's the internet is built by love. When one region is touched either positive or negative, the effect resonates and ripples through the entire web.

In closing I'd like say this to every woman who might stumble to this book. It seems that a lot of men have lost the ability to show you respect However, simply because we've done it earned it, don't let that mean you lose respect for yourself. Be a true king. You truly are Mother Earth. You breathe life and fill our planet. You make our bleak world beautiful. You embody your Essence of the Divine and love that is a part of our entire world. You are much more powerful and more valuable than what we've been treating you with, telling you about, and teaching you. Don't be a slave to our nonsense. Because most of us people have put our crowns onto the ground, and have picked up the jester's scepter, make sure take off your crown from your head. You are the life of the party. Your love is unconditional. You are wise. Your truth should not remain hidden. Say what you believe and be the manifestation of your goals. We Kings will eventually meet you there.

Chapter 15: The Mindset Can Be The Most Important

"Instead of stressing about the things you can't be in control of,

Your focus should be on the possibilities of what you can make."

- Roy T. Bennett

The main goal for creating a profitable business is to be a leader by example and instilling your employees to follow suit. Positive mindsets are the most effective tool you can employ to push yourself to higher levels. Your thoughts create your world, both inside and outside When you focus your attention on positive thinking you'll see that it has ripple effects throughout your professional and personal life. There are many methods to change your perspective so that you are able to push through and reach your full potential.

If you concentrate on positive thoughts, it could also be beneficial to use affirmations to yourself. This tactic is utilized by military forces as well as business leaders in high-stress situations. If you can boost your self-esteem by delivering a motivational speech, you will significantly boost your self-confidence.

Contrarily, if constantly focusing your mind to negative thoughts, you're likely to observe an underlying pattern. You'll see that your life is stained through these feelings. You may begin to experience physical reactions due to the negative thoughts that are internalizing their thoughts.

If this occurs it's possible for physical ailments to trigger. In reality the cause of illness is an imbalance of your spiritual, mental or physical aspects of your. Many people recognize the reasons why someone is sick. If you are feeling negative in your body, you're not likely to be able to see all the positive things frequently within your physical environment. What you will be able to see is the negative feelings you experience inside.

This is exactly the result of focused on negative thoughts. Imagine the impact from positive thought on body. It's the other aspect of the spectrum. You can reverse the negative effects of negative thoughts with patience and persistence. You can feel more positive through positive thinking. This is the reason it's been so well-known as time passes; people are beginning to realize the advantages of controlling their minds. It's not much simpler than saying the same phrase over and over again each day.

I touched on the idea in the previous section that positive affirmations can be an effective method of directing your thoughts towards a positive direction when you begin your day. The way you start your first half hour the day is likely determine the direction for the rest days. If you wake up in a hurry or concerned about a meeting you have later in the day, it's going set the tone for facing the problems for the rest of your day. But, if you do make your alarm and rise on time, perhaps even earlier than you normally do and you'll be more calm and focused to tackle the day ahead.

The Fundamentals of Affirmations

Utilizing affirmations to begin of the day is crucial in getting you into an optimistic mindset, however it does not have to be solely focused on the morning. You can use these affirmations throughout the day. There's no limit on the number of pep talk messages you can offer you throughout your day in order to keep your thoughts focussed on positive outcomes in any situation that might occur. The more you incorporate affirmations into your life, the greater the impact they'll affect your thoughts throughout the day.

One way you can ensure that your mind stays engaged all day long is to have an affirmation or quote that inspires you to be at a central location at work or at home. The affirmation must be an effective phrase that stimulates your blood flow and makes you push your limits to become the best possible you could be. It has to be something you have faith in your heart and can help you through any situation. It could be a phrase that you've carried around with you for the duration of your life or something you have read recently that resonates with you . It provides you with the motivation that you need to continue working toward your objectives.

You can focus in particular to your affirmation. You can have it professionally printed and framed in a way that it grabs your attention during the course of your day. It could be hung in the room by your computer, or put at your desk where you work. It will be like a friend who is always around to provide the direction and support you require. When your thoughts wandering and you are worried about the situation take a look at your dependable confirmation and remember the goals you're trying to accomplish throughout the day. You'll be amazed by how quickly it will bring your attention back to the present and provide direction again. Remember that occasionally the affirmation you are chanting can out of use as you become used to hearing it. If you discover this to be an issue, you can modify your affirmations and make them printed on a different colour paper, to attract your attention or put the picture in a different frame to ensure that it pops out more clearly.

Another method you can use to incorporate affirmations into your daily routine is to write them on your calendar for different times throughout the day. Perhaps you've got a planned timetable to complete a difficult project , or maybe you get sluggish during the afternoon. If you put these affirmations to be a reminder on your smartphone or calendar on your computer, you'll be able to get a boost of energy during the moments when they will be useful to keep your mind to your best goals.

It is also possible to create teams or support buddies. It can be easily created by creating a group using Facebook Messenger, WhatsApp, or any other chat or social media tools. Members will continue to share inspirational messages throughout the day, ensuring that each member of the group will benefit. It is possible to create an online platform to send emails for the group, so that occasionally you can share more powerful messages of encouragement which are too long for the size of a text message. When you are surrounded by positive individuals as well as messages during the entire day It will provide you with the confidence to reach any goal you've set for yourself for the day.

If you are finding that you aren't aware of some inspiring quotes or phrases that you like, browse the internet for inspiration because they are available on sites and memes posted on social networks. Every site offers a method to save these quotes on your account, or on your phone or desktop. Slideshows can be created of these saved images. It's also a simpler option to print them to be able to display them on prominent locations of your office or home.

Self-improvement books that inspire you and famous quotes could be a great method to discover phrases that speak to your heart. Being aware that there's always something to learn can make you more of a person. If you are determined to study or learn something new each day, it gives you the chance to develop professionally and personally in a rapid manner. You can look up inspiring books on the internet and talk to your support group about the books and websites they have read to find motivation.

For additional sources of motivation Begin by surrounded yourself with people who can inspire you. If you believe you've got everything done, you shut yourself off from the valuable information you could gain from other people. Join a social club or catch up with a family or friend member as often as is feasible to talk about the things you've learned or are learning between your gatherings. If you are exposed to stories of the things that other people do in their field or in their lives, it lets you think about the ways you can apply what they've taken away to your own. This way, you'll be able to gain from their mistakes and lessons to begin to make a start on making improvements and empowering yourself throughout your life.

Always be to learn. There is always a way we can grow and improve ourselves, which will impact our lives in many, but not all aspects that we live in. Any small change in your daily routine or thoughts could have a ripple effect. This being said be sure to consider any possibility that could assist you in achieving your goals. towards your goals. You won't be aware of how beneficial they could be until you have tried. Be open-minded and mindful of people and situations that you meet in your day-to-day life as there's always something you can learn from the people you encounter, even if recognize that they are giving you the example for what you should not do.

If you are in a challenging situation, there's no reason to avoid from the negative experiences that you have had within your life. These challenges can aid you in your growth as an person, and it all depends on the way you think. If you can simply change your viewpoint when in these situations, you will gain a deeper understanding of your own situation and yourself. Instead of asking "Why does this happen for me?" and turning it into "Why does this happen to myself?" you can gain greater insight.

The way you think about it will not only help this approach help you let go of thinking of your self as victim, but it will also allow you to gain control over the circumstances. The ability to relax and take a look at the bigger perspective will allow you to avoid being back in this situation or at minimum, give you knowledge of how to deal with any similar situations later on. It is time to stop making excuses and dwelling on the negative and instead, take the path of consciousness. This gives you the leg up you require to to overcome any obstacle you encounter when you strive to achieve your maximum potential.

The science behind Daily Affirmations

There have also been numerous scientific studies that have been conducted on the ways that affirmations and positive thoughts can bring significant shifts and transformations in negative and unhealthy thought patterns. The first scientific study , conducted in 1988 formulated The Self-Affirmation Theory which is based on three major aspects:

Each person is a part of a larger story about themselves that they can affirm through self-affirmation

* The requirement to be knowledgeable about the values that each person has is what makes them a great person

A person's actions are rewarded with praise

Through the story that you create for yourself, you form your self-image. It also shapes your perception that you're capable of adapting, and that you are moral as well as flexible. Due to your capacity to change and adapt the self-identity you have also these characteristics. It's not a predetermined notion like "mother" or "daughter." It is more of a self-identity is what you think of yourself as a person in various identity and roles.

In addition, by consolidating your self-esteem and sustaining the conviction that you are moral and good in various circumstances. This doesn't mean you have to be exceptional or extraordinary to feel confident about your self-image It is more about how you view yourself in various roles and situations , and the way you respond.

These actions are your way to show your integrity. These are not actions you do to attract attention or boost your ego. Actually, you are taking these actions because they reflect your values and beliefs and reflect your true self. If you can recognize the core of what you're about then you can use the self-affirmation concept to improve your mental state. (Cascio)

If you can be true to yourself, you'll keep growing and strengthening your self-esteem. This will bring you a greater satisfaction and a sense of purpose that will spread to the other areas within your daily life. It's the gift that you give yourself that keeps giving. You will be more in tune with your own self that will inspire you to continue to push toward your goals. The only limits you face are those you set through your thought process. If you can see that this is not the case, you'll be able to continue climbing up and up.

Since the creation of the self-affirmation theory, researchers have been studying the neuroscience field to determine if there is physical changes to the brain after using affirmations to shift your thinking process between positive and negative cycles. These tests were performed using MRI scans to find out the neural pathways affected when people were being examined were repeatedly reciting affirmations. The conclusion was that the brain's prefrontal cortex that is linked to positive appraisal, was more active when engaged in affirmation exercises. (Falk)

The affirmations are intended to change your mind's programming to become more positive, and this can be an effective thought process in itself. If you can decrease your negative thoughts, you are less likely to think about the negative experiences you could have thought about prior to implementing daily affirmations. (Wiesenfeld)

When you stop focused on negative thoughts or experiences in exchange for positive thoughts, you're capable of creating positive narratives that can be adapted to who you are and the goals you set out to achieve.

If you've never tried affirmations for yourself that are positive you should be aware that there aren't specific rules regarding the is the best time or frequency at which they should be spoken. If you're capable of identifying the negative thoughts patterns that you often fall into, you can employ affirmation methods to alter these patterns of thought and turn them into

Conclusion

It's safe, but sad to acknowledge it is one of the major dangers of the 21st century everywhere world is the effect of gender inequality, and the way it is progressively decreasing and hindering us and preventing us from going in the proper direction to grow. Also, it is true that we as well as the entire world are not in a position to finding a lasting solution to this problem and are merely throwing fuel to the flames.

The gender gap has turned into a reason for anger and competition. We have been shaming one another, and that has sent us all on the streets, firing guns at our natural opponents. In contrast to taking measures to stop the issue, we slack off our hands, surrounded by a mockery and banter that is full of hatred to the term equality. We haven't yet begun looking at ways to coexist in a harmonious way. There is no doubt that gender inequality is the second most discriminatory factor after racial across the globe. Every time you hear a conversation that is that is trending, you can find gender inequality and racism from its origins.

My mind is convinced that women to be captivating in the way they were designed naturally. Numerous studies have proven that women are more educated than males. Also, taking into consideration how well-crafted their minds are and the way they perform well, and it's is more flattering for women to realize that they have been designed to handle the stress of carrying out a multitude of tasks simultaneously. Women can be found at home washing dishes, cooking and cleaning and efficiently and in time to enjoy her favorite TV shows. Men can't do it without being stretched too much. It's just one tiny evidence of how women, if given the chance to succeed can help make the world better. We'll return for a short digression to understand why I believe the urgent need for women to become equipped and be given the same experiences like any other human being, regardless of gender.

All of this raises the question: why women need to be empowered? How do women become empowered? and how can empowerment for women transform the entire world.

I believe that the most fundamental and most sensible way to discuss these issues is to examine the extent to which inequality has violated the fundamental female rights. Since I believe that women shouldn't be able to even ask to be empowered and empowered, they should be walking effortlessly and free of charge on empowerment just as every other man with a right to be. I believe that the initial steps towards empowerment should come from allowing these God-given rights to be a success.